CONTENTS

MAPS IN THE GUIDEBOOK
(116 A1) Page numbers and
coordinates refer to the street
atlas and the overview map
of Lisbon and surroundings
on p. 134/135
(0) Site/address located off
the map. Coordinates are
also given for places that are
not marked in the city atlas.
You'll find a network map for
public transport in the back
flap

**INSIDE BACK COVER:
PULL-OUT MAP →**

PULL-OUT MAP 🔎
(⨂ A–B 2–3) Refers to the
removable pull-out map

The best MARCO POLO Insider Tips

Our top 15 Insider Tips

INSIDER TIP **Beach clubs on the Tagus**
Relax in one of the terrace bars along the riverbank. Sip a beer, watch the passing boats and let your thoughts wander → p. 27

INSIDER TIP **Jungle in the City**
Called *estufas*, these hothouses filled with tropical plants and pools, butterflies and geckos form an oasis of calm in the big city bustle → p. 36

INSIDER TIP **Stroll in lofty heights**
Enjoy panoramic views from the 'Aqueduct of the Free Waters', which supplied the city with water from the mid-18th century to 1967 → p. 50

INSIDER TIP **A taste of rural Portugal**
Catch the Metro to the charmingly old-fashioned bairro of Carnide and sample traditional rustic fare at *O Miudinho* restaurant → p. 65

INSIDER TIP **Literary Lisbon!**
Literary minds will enjoy exchanging ideas with João Pimentel, the knowledgeable owner of the *Fábula Urbis* bookshop specialising in Lisbon and Portugal. Stock up on novels, poetry and cookbooks – many in English → p. 68

INSIDER TIP **Chill out with the alternative scene**
The *Miradouro de Santa Catarina* is a great place to come after a night spent dancing. Enjoy the view and recharge in the sun – a spot of private street entertainment is usually thrown in (photo r.) → p. 41

INSIDER TIP **Morna instead of fado**
The Portuguese have fado, the inhabitants of the Cape Verde islands have morna. The *Casa de Morna* offers music, dance and good food. Enjoy specialities from the former Portuguese colony → p. 63

BEST OF ...

FOR FREE

● *Greenery, scenery...*

Lisbon has no shortage of pretty and freely accessible beauty spots. The labyrinthine garden of the *Museu de Calouste Gulbenkian* is a favourite with couples for *namorar* (romantic assignments), for impromptu picnics and to while away the hours reading (photo) → p. 51

● *Low-cost city tours*

Leaving from the Largo de Camões, a new generation of city guides have introduced a new concept – tip-based (instead of fee-based) tours → p. 103

● *Tile-watching*

On any stroll through the city, you'll come across Portuguese tiles – Art Nouveau designs, tiles incorporating a telling phrase, and even 3D effects in tiles. On Sunday morning (up to 2pm), the *Museu do Azulejo* lets visitors in for free → p. 52

● *Parque das Nações*

Pull on your trainers, set off along the Mar de Palha ('Sea of Straw'), and tick off the attractions: Santiago Calatrava's Oriente train station, outdoor sculptures and the Garden of the Colonies. The state spent a lot of money creating the site for Expo '98, so you might as well enjoy it – it's free → p. 53

● *Cork carvings*

Baroque sculptor Joaquim Castro de Machado was a master of the typically Portuguese art of carving nativity scenes out of cork. Admire one of his largest works, featuring hundreds of figurines, inside the *Basílica da Estrela* – for free → p. 43

● *Free museum visits*

Top museums such as the *Museu do Oriente* offer free entry at certain times, usually until 2pm on Sundays. At the Jesuit church and museum *São Roque*, you can join a free tour in English at 3pm → p. 52, 41

●●●● Dots in guidebook refer to 'Best of ...' tips

● *Terraces with a view*

Lisboetas, like tourists, are forever hunting the best view of the city and Tagus river. One of the finest vantage points is the *Miradouro São Pedro de Alcântara* looking across to the Old Town and Castelo → p. 42

● *Coffee culture*

Students and office workers, elderly ladies and Atlantic coast surfers: they all share one habit – stopping for a coffee at any opportunity. The most famous and atmospheric place for this is the *Café a Brasileira* in Chiado (photo) → p. 58

● *Happy to be sad*

You'll hear fado, the 'Portuguese blues', with its undertones of melancholy and longing, on every corner in Lisbon. Don't miss a live performance in one of the atmospheric fado venues → p. 20, 78

● *A Streetcar named Nostalgia*

The old-fashioned yellow trams are used by tourists and citizens alike. The No. 28 offers the best ride in town, rumbling up through narrow alleys, inches the houses → p. 26

● *Stay on the ball*

Everybody knows that the people who brought us Figo and Ronaldo are football-mad. At the local derby between Benfica (red) and Sporting (green) things get pretty heated. But even 'regular' league games are always worth a party → p. 34

● *Look down*

Lisbon's famous *calçada,* pavements laid by skilled craftsmen, occasionally take on fabulous shapes and forms. Cast your eyes over the wave patterns on Rossio square or the phallic representations between the Brasileira café and the Benetton store in Chiado → p. 39

● *Up the town and down the town*

One of Lisbon's icons are the *elevadores,* funiculars and lifts that have been transporting people up to Chiado and the Bairro Alto for over 100 years. A new one is being built in 2012 to ease access to the Castle. Don't miss being whizzed uptown in the cast-iron tower of the *Elevador de Santa Justa*! → p. 35

ONLY IN

BEST OF ...

● **Sea creatures**
At the Oceanarium, Europe's second-largest aquarium, wet afternoons pass quickly among the sharks, marine turtles and sun fish → p. 53, 96

● **Coach Museum**
With its splendid historic coaches, the *Museu Nacional dos Coches* in Belém is the most popular museum in Lisbon. In 2013, the museum moves into its ambitious 'hovering' new home (photo) → p. 48

● **From port to port**
The *Solar do Vinho do Porto* is a classic space for tasting port wine at fair prices. Order an aromatic *azeitão* cheese, to spoon out and spread on slices of bread – very tasty! → p. 73

● **Temple of books**
Fábula Úrbis is arguably the best bookshop in town, and a great place for book-lovers to while away a rainy hour or two. Pick up a coffee from upstairs and browse its excellent selection of English-language titles → p. 68

● **Shopping in style**
Join those lisboetas who refuse to let the economic crisis ruin their love of shopping. Enjoy the shops and people-watching below the postmodern towers of *Amoreiras* or in the mega *Centro Comercial Colombo* → p. 68

● **Hip culture**
Today, it's ideas rather than textiles that are produced at *LX Factory*. There's a pizzeria, a cool bookshop with a space for experimental music, designer shops, event s and clubs → p. 80

RAIN

RELAX AND CHILL OUT
Take it easy and spoil yourself

● *Pole position*
Many trendy terrace cafés such as the *Esplanada das Portas do Sol* have comfy sofas and beanbags on which to chill out. The Indian-influenced *Lost In* terrace even offers a bed with a view over the city → **p. 33, 93**

● *Float away*
Let the saline solution in the floating tank at *Float In* carry you into a state of complete relaxation. → **p. 22**

● *Experience Belém in peace and quiet*
The Hieronymite Monastery in Belém draws the tourists like bees to a honeypot. Come early, at 10am, to catch the magical peace of the cloisters without the crowds → **p. 46**

● *Kick back on the beach*
Even in spring or autumn it is usually warm enough to sit by the sea, or even take a dip. Don't worry about organising a picnic hamper, just sit yourself down in one of the many beach cafés lining the *Costa Caparica* → **p. 48**

● *Go with the flow*
Board a Tagus ferry or a river cruising boat and lean back, enjoying the wonderful views of the city from the water → **p. 27, 103**

● *Palace garden*
Spoil yourself with a massage and other spa treatments in the *Garden Spa* of the *Pestana Palace Hotel*, overlooking the splendid gardens of a 19th-century palace → **p. 22**

● *Uplifting reading*
Grab your holiday reading and climb up to the *Castelo de São Jorge* (photo). Afterwards, find a quiet spot in this extensive complex to read your book and soak up the fabulous city views – sheer balm for the soul! → **p. 30**

DISCOVER LISBON!

The Sleeping Beauty on the Tagus, Lisbon is steeped in the irresistible charm of times past. Magnificent palaces and monasteries bear witness to colonial riches; picturesque alleyways and staircases, pretty corners and sleepy squares enchant visitors. That's not all though: the melancholy capital on the southwestern edge of Europe has another side that is dynamic, modern and cosmopolitan. Young hipsters party in the smart riverbank clubs and restaurants or get their kicks from bar-hopping in the party neighbourhood of Bairro Alto – and increasingly around the port of Cais de Sodré. Lisbon, once the capital of a large chunk of the world, today represents a melting pot of cultures. Lisbon – Lisboa (pronounced 'lishbóa') in Portuguese – is both metropolitan and provincial, multicultural and open to the world, welcoming and relaxed. 'Live and let live' is the motto here. The city and its inhabitants are imbued with a certain spirit of laissez-faire, which accompanies the much-referenced *saudade*. Considered the key to the soul of the Portuguese, this melancholy way of being is difficult to capture in words.

Photo: view across the city from Parque Eduardo VII

Lisbon's heart still beats around Rossio. Feel the pulse of urban life on this grand central square, with its mosaic pavement and terrace cafés. The whole of Lisbon life can be seen here: briefcase-wielding suits, chic shoppers in designer outfits, teenagers with their phones stuck to their ear, groups of Africans deep in gesticulating discussion, shoe shiners bent over businessmen's loafers, lottery ticket sellers, and street vendors advertising their business. Taking pride of place above the city is the medieval Castelo de São Jorge. The traditional Alfama neighbourhood below the castle is a picturesque maze of alleyways and winding staircases, redolent of times long past – and fragrant with the smell of grilled sardines. Skew-whiff walls gnarled by the passage of time shelter small bars *(tascas)*, grocery and bric-a-brac shops. Faded tiles *(azulejos)* adorn walls and arches. Just as they did 100 years ago, the trams *(eléctricos)* trundle up and down the hills, past houses with small birdcages hanging in the windows and washing drying in the wind.

Liberal and cosmopolitan – live and let live

Opposite the castle, the Chiado quarter epitomises Lisbon elegance. This is where the city's first theatres, academies of fine art and architecture and colleges of dance and music are located. While the Chiado fire of 1988 shocked lisboetas, it also offered the chance to inject fresh new life into the quarter. Architect Álvaro Vieira Silva will

Popular for a stroll around the Baixa – Rua Augusta leads down to the Tagus

forever be connected with the rebuilding of the Chiado. From Rossio, walk through the Baixa (Downtown) towards the river, past the window displays of designer boutiques and quaint little shops. Street musicians and ambulant vendors popu-

From the Upper Town to the banks of the Tagus

late the pedestrian promenade, which ends at the magnificent Praça do Comércio. The glittering waters of the Tagus – a lot cleaner since the introduction of a new treatment plant – are plied by colourful ferryboats. Occasionally the monotone horn of an ocean liner is a reminder that the Atlantic is just down the road. Seen from the river, and particularly in the warm glow of the late afternoon, Lisbon appears like an Impressionist painting – in tones of ochre, dotted with church towers and domes.

In 1994, Lisbon was Europe's Capital of Culture, and in 1998 it presented the last World Exposition of the 20th century, a successful event that Lisbon is still benefiting from today. The Expo and the 2004 UEFA European Football Championship brought massive urban renewal. Whole new areas emerged, old neighbourhoods were transformed, and slums torn down. Today, Lisbon is a city of fascinating juxtapositions. You'll find avant garde towers rising amid medieval residential quarters, American-inspired shopping alongside the old-fashioned shops of the Baixa, where vendors have all the time in the world to measure out fabric or weigh out coffee from

Portugal's former colonies. Crumbling façades hide designer stores and fancy discos; hip clubs and fine restaurants occupy old warehouses on the banks of the Tagus, and up-to-the minute bars and chic shops have taken root in the party quarter of Bairro Alto.

Lisbon has about 500,000 inhabitants, Greater Lisbon some two million. The city is a melting pot of cultures. In the 1960s and '70s, hundreds of thousands of immigrants from Portugal's former African colonies such as Angola and Mozambique arrived, as well as Portuguese retornados, and are now well integrated in Portuguese society. Immigrants from Brazil, India (Goa) and China and Pakistan have settled in areas such as Martim Moniz and are also a fixture of the capital's urban image.

According to one legend, Lisbon was founded by Odysseus. The city took off under the Romans, who settled the estuary of the River Tagus in 205 BC and turned Olissopona into Lusitania's most important marketplace. Tangible testimonies from that time are the ruins of the Roman theatre (Teatro Romano) in Alfama, today a museum. A more lasting influence on the city was provided by the Moors, who conquered Lisbon in 714. During their 400-year rule, Lisbon became a centre of Arabic culture, and saw the emergence of the Alfama and Mouraria neighbourhoods, then unfortified suburbs, today in the heart of the city.

In 1147, King Dom Afonso Henriques managed to reconquer the city, with the help of the Crusaders. Lisbon became the seat of the royal family, and with the end of the Christian reconquest (Reconquista) in the 13th century the capital of the young Portuguese kingdom. The city reached its true glory in the 15th and 16th centuries, the Age of Discovery, when Portuguese seafarers explored the world. In 1488, Bartolomeu Diaz rounded the Cape of Good Hope. Ten years later, Vasco da Gama discovered the sea route to India, and shortly after that, Pedro Álvares Cabral landed in Brazil. Soon this tiny country boasted a world empire, and Lisbon became the most magnificent capital in Europe. Ships laden with gold and silver, spices and precious woods – and slaves – laid anchor at the port, and the flourishing trade brought the capital immeasurable wealth. Splendid buildings such as the Hieronymus Monastery (Mosteiro dos Jerónimos) in the suburb of Belém underlined Lisbon's role as a centre of world trade.

Glorious past

The Golden Era came to an abrupt end with a devastating earthquake in November 1755. The disaster took just a few hours to bring rack and ruin to the city, as well as claiming more than 40,000 the lives. The foreign minister at the time, Marquês de Pombal, also turned out to be an urban planner of genius, meticulously plotting its rebirth on the drawing board. Straight streets, clear lines, 90-degree angles, a safety margin between the rows of houses – the Pombalina or Baixa was born.

Decades of economic and political turbulence ensued. The royal family became mired in intermarriages and failed to produce any more monarchs of note. In 1910, King Manuel II fled Portugal for Britain following a coup d'état. The country became a Republic, and then a dictatorship. The fascist dictator António de Oliveira Salazar held on to the reins of power for nearly half a century – Europe's longest dictatorship. While he managed to keep Portugal out of the World War II, he also turned it into the 'poorhouse of Europe' (Salazar's own words). The police state was swept away on 25 April 1974 by a peaceful revolt by generals despairing of the colonial wars. This had the support of the people and was known the 'Carnation Revolution' – named after the red carnations (cravos) placed in the muzzles of soldiers' rifles. Joining the European Community (now the EU) in 1986 gave the country a new-found confidence, but many obsolete structures remained in place.

The usual big-city problems haven't spared Lisbon either. The international port is a gateway for drugs coming into Europe, and the periphery of the city has its share of very poor neighbourhoods. The republic's centenary on 5 October 2010 fell in the middle of the current economic crisis. Today's harsh realities include 12 per cent unemployment, low productivity, record emigration – and since 2011 strict structural reforms imposed by the IMF. This means major infrastructure project such as the new airport have been put on hold. Lisboetas themselves have had to make many personal economies. In March 2011, a demonstration convened by *Geração À Rasca* – literally 'the generation that has nothing', or 'fed up' – united hundreds of thousands of people along the Avenida da Liberdade. The protests were partly aimed at the lack of job opportunities for graduates and government corruption.

The present: difficult times

Modern Lisbon: roof of Oriente Station and the Vasco da Gama shopping centre

Meanwhile, Lisbon remains a fascinating destination for visitors. Again and again, unusual vistas appear: pristinely dressed Russian sailors sitting on a bench; black-robed students reciting verses and singing in the streets; a young girl in a scarlet crinoline dress on her way to a protest march. If there's one golden rule for visitors to Lisbon, it's never forget your camera! Apart from the Expo area, now known as Parque das Nações (Park of Nations), and the suburb of Belém, with its plethora of museums and grandiose monuments, Lisbon's main sights lie quite close together. Even the hills have been tamed to a certain degree by the funiculars, *elevadores and eléctricos*. Wear a good pair of shoes, keep your eyes open and bring a good dose of patience – that's all you need to get to know Lisbon and its people.

WHAT'S HOT

1 Sugar rush

Watch the calories Lisboetas have a sweet tooth, and especially love cakes. *Betycat* makes fabulous cakes – in the shape of Lisbon's sights *(betycat.blogspot.com)*. *Hand Mania* cakes are made by hand using regional ingredients *(handmania-bolos.blogspot.com)*. *Pastéis de Cerveja* bakes with beer, following an ancient secret recipe *(Rua de Belém 15–17)*. Simply delicious!

Eyecatcher

Fashion Miles of fabric are turned into eminently wearable works of sartorial art at *Storytailors (Calçada do Ferragial 8, www.storytailors. pt, photo)*. Alexandra Moura's range *(Rua Dom Pedro V 77, www.alexandramoura.com)* is more sober, while Ricardo Dourado's designs have a futuristic touch *(from Akira, Calçada do Combro 8, ricardodourado.blogspot.com)*. Dino Alves tailors clothes for men and women. His speciality: provocative unisex pieces *(www.dinoalves.eu)*.

2

3 The ultimate sport

Latest craze A new kind of frisbee is currently invading Lisbon's airspace, as the team sport Beach Ultimate becomes more and more popular. Want to take part in the fun? Head for the small beach at Belém *(information on place and times: sports.groups.yahoo.com/group/bug-lisboa)*. Those wanting to buy a disc so they can play on the beach at home should check out *Discos Voadores (Rua Palmira 66)*. The *Liga Lisboa* brings together local teams *(for dates, see www.bug-p.org, photo)*.

Scoot off

Getting around the city Buggies, scooters or a Segway? Sightseeing on Lisbon's seven hills doesn't have to result in sore feet. Visitors to Lisbon looking for a different way to get around are spoilt for choice. And nobody needs to worry about carbon emissions. The vehicles are powered by electricity, and on request the integrated GPS will tell you about the sights along the way. *(Rua dos Fanqueiros 9.30am–1pm, 2–6.30pm, 7.30pm in summer, www.redtourgps.com, photo). Go Car Tours* has electric two-seaters, also fitted with GPS *(Rua Douradores 16, www.gocartours.pt).* Another Segway provider is *Go Segway Tours (Doca de Alcântara, www.gosegwaytours.com).*

Etch-a-sketch

Grave matters Over 500 years ago, Europe was gripped by a new artistic trend. Etchings and copper engravings were in vogue – only to fall into oblivion again a few years later. In Lisbon, a group of young creatives has revived the art, called *gravura* in Portugal. The *Contraprova atelier (contraprova-gravura.blogspot.com)* is situated in the *Atelier de Artistas Gravadores (Rua do Garrido 62),* which also offers workshops in the labour-intensive technique. One of the hottest representatives of the new art form is Lisbon-based Joanna Latka *(joannalatka-exibitions.blogspot.com, photo). The Galeria Salgadeiras* regularly shows works by practitioners of the art, and Latka herself has exhibited in this gallery space *(Rua das Salgadeiras 24, www.salgadeiras.com).*

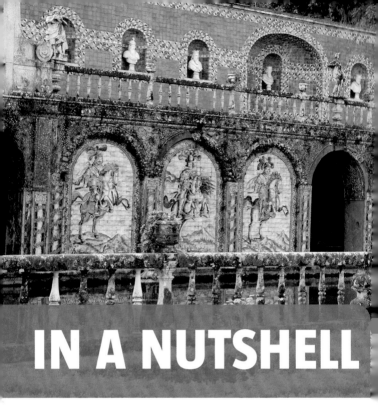

IN A NUTSHELL

A ZULEJOS

Azulejos (pronounced: azoolay-shoosh) can bee seen everywhere in Lisbon. The colourful tiles adorn the walls of houses and benches, staircases and arches. The art of tiling is part of the city's Moorish heritage, and the name is derived from the Arabic *al zulaique* ('small polished stone'). Tiled landscapes and scenes of daily life tell a lot about Portugal's history and culture. The *Museu Nacional do Azulejo* gives an excellent overview of the history of the tiled images. And a new generation of tile artists is treading new paths, choosing unusual motifs or employing the art in new ways – replicate a minimalist trend at home with a single tiny tile on its own on a big wall ...

B IKING

Lisbon's cyclists are starting to stake a claim on the city streets, very gently; if you want to meet them, hire a bike on the last Friday of the month, get yourself to the central Marquês de Pombal roundabout and join the *Massa Crítica (www.massacriticapt.net)*, where a couple of dozen lisboetas reclaim the street for themselves. The whole thing is done in polite Portuguese style: one lane is left free for motorised traffic. The city authorities are slowly increasing the number of cycle paths. Be aware, though, that the grooves of the *eléctricos* are death traps for cyclists, who also have to deal with the contempt of bus and taxi drivers.

Photo: Azulejo images from the Palacio dos Marqueses de Fronteira

Saints, colourful tiles, fashion, daily life in Lisbon – and, of course, fado, the Portuguese blues

DAILY LIFE

Many visitors on short city trips meet only waiters and shop assistants, but it is worth taking the time to examine society more closely: how do lisboetas live today? The pace here is certainly slower than in other European capitals. If you know the London rush hour, the Metro will appear a cosy coffee party to you. Coffee rather than tea: lisboetas celebrate their coffee culture and take time out to spend with their friends, the *convivio*.

Statistically, compared with their European counterparts, the Portuguese are among the latest to go to bed, and have the most difficulty getting up in the morning. While the Portuguese have the second-longest working hours in Europe after the British, their productivity doesn't match the hours they put in. To some extent, the older generation is still in thrall to fatalism, paired with a love of gambling that has no match in Europe. Evidence of the lisboetas' passion for football is everywhere.

Lisbon's city centre is losing inhabitants. Couples with children soon realise how difficult it is to push a buggy up and down the steep, cobblestoned streets. Popular alternatives are the chic avenidas or the nicer suburbs, even though the neighbourhood feel is very different

ELÉCTRICOS

For over 100 years, the wonderfully old-fashioned tramways have been trundling around the city, squeaking and groaning. Many of the old lines are no longer in use, and modern trams have replaced some of the vintage ones. For

Fado as a tool of seduction – this painting hangs in the Museu do Fado

there – for example, the modern *condominios* may not permit their occupants to hang washing outside the windows. It's mostly young foreigners who enjoy moving into the characterful (though usually modernised) apartments of the Old Town. They are prepared to put up with tumbledown façades and signs of social deprivation outside their front door in return for the charm of living in a bairro histórico.

the CARRIS company, the historic vehicles are hardly worth maintaining, but the tradition-loving lisboetas are fighting for their survival. The picturesque funiculars and the *Elevador de Santa Justa* tend to serve the tourists more than the locals.

FADO AND MORE

Fado is the Portuguese blues. It was born in the poor neighbourhoods of Lisbon, Alfama and Mouraria in the second half of the 18th century, and for a long time had a disreputable reputation. The word is derived from the Latin *fatum* (fate). While both men and women *(fadistas)* sing the fado, it is always accompanied by two men, usually with stoic expressions, working two string instruments, a twelve-string guitar and a kind of lute, the *guitarra portuguesa*. In terms of subject matter, the fado revolves around love, Lisbon, hope and disappointment – and most of all the *saudade* (see below), a distinctly Portuguese feeling. What fado means to the Portuguese was evident in 1999, when Amália Rodrigues, the 'Queen of Fado', died. A three-day period of state mourning was declared. Amália's house in the Rua de São Bento (Nos. 191–193) has become a pilgrimage site for her fans *(Tue– Sun 10am–1pm and 2–6pm | admission 5 euros | Metro (yellow) Rato)*. To this day, nobody can compare with the goddess of fado, but there are many new names on the scene, such as Camané and the internationally successful Mariza.

Many visitors to the city hear fado for the first time as a canned version, emanating from a green fadomobile in Rua do Carmo. Lisbon's only ambulant music vendor acquired the right to sell music on the street after losing his record store in the devastating fire that destroyed Chiado in 1988. When the area was rebuilt rents skyrocketed. Young stars such as the Sara Tavares, of Cape Verdean heritage, and the strong-voiced Cristina Branco and Ana Moura have breathed new life into the genre.

Come in June for the celebrations honouring the patron saints and you won't be able to ignore the other great popular music tradition in Portugal: *pimba,* accordion-supported songs with unequivocally equivocal lyrics. Lisbon's Cape Verdeans sing their heartfelt *morna* – you might know the late Cesaria Evora's successful ballad 'Saudade'. The Angolan community likes to dance the *kuduro,* a slighty hectic but eminently danceable sound. Portugal's internationally successful kuduro band is Buraka Som Sistema from the poor suburb of Amadora. The most famous club for those sounds is *Mussulo (www.discotecamussulo.com),* named after a beach strip near Luanda. Both kuduro and the calmer *kizomba* have a slightly macho image, with music videos featuring besuited, sunglass-wearing guys and swooning ladies in bikinis.

FASHION

While the lisboetas enjoy fashion, their sense of style is not over the top and often displays a very personal touch. Young women like to pep up their look with fun details – you'll see many oversized sunglasses peeping through curtains of (mostly long) hair. In the summer, both men and women slip their feet into Brazilian *Havaiana* flip flops – Lisbon's cobbles make short shrift of high heels. Middle-aged ladies often like to wear colour-coordinated attire, and the famous *tias* (ladies who lunch) from the area around Cascais like to go about their busy high society lives in pearls and a permatan. Heterosexual men tend to wear either a suit or T-shirt and jeans, or pleated trousers and a shirt. Well-known Lisbon names on the international fashion scene are Ana Salazar, Fatima Lopes and José António Tenente.

MANUELINE STYLE

Manueline style is a Portuguese variant of Flamboyant Gothic. This decorative, playful style, named after King Manuel I (1495–1521), was introduced in the early 16th century. Inspired by the exotic adventures of the seafarers and maritime explorers of the time, the architects and stonemasons covered their buildings with delicate carvings of ropes and knots, exotic plants and animals, shells and fish. For particularly beautiful examples of this architectural style, don't miss the Hieronymus Monastery in Belém.

PATRON SAINTS

Lisbon's official patron saint is São Vicente, a martyr whose body was guided safely to Lisbon on a rudderless boat from the Cabo de São Vicente on the Algarve by a pair of ravens. However, the alfacinhas – 'little lettuces' – venerate their true patron saint, Santo António, much more than São Vicente. Born in 1195 in Lisbon, Santo António spent most of his life as a preacher and Franciscan monk in France and Italy, dying in 1231 in a monastery near Padua (elsewhere in the world he is venerated as St Antonius of Padua). The saint is credited with numerous miracles, and is the patron saint of lovers and the poor, as well as the forgetful.

For the older generation in Portugal at least, religion plays a major role. Around 90 per cent of the population are Roman-Catholic. On feast days, statues of saints such as Our Lady of the Pains are carried through the city in processions, flanked by the lavender-carrying faithful. One Pope declared the Portuguese to be 'the most religious people in the world'. However, the umbrella of Catholicism encompasses many ancient customs and rites, forming an eclectic mix of religious belief and superstition. People vow great devotion to their favourite saint, and every problem has a patron saint who can sort it out. Santa Lúcia helps with eye complaints, São Braz with colds, São Pedro is in charge of the fishermen, São Roque cures warts. In some neighbourhoods, you'll see shop windows full of votive candles to guard against the evil eye or financial ruin alongside statuettes of Nossa Senhora da Fátima. On top of that, Brazilian and Angolan immigrants have imported their own eclectic customs.

PESSOA

Lisboetas have commemorated Fernando Pessoa (1888–1935), probably Portugal's most famous poet, with a bronze monument in front of his favourite café, *A Brasileira*. Today, few of the countless tourists who have their picture

RELAX & CHILL OUT

The uncrowned queen among Lisbon's spas is the ● *Garden Spa* at the *Pestana Palace Hotel*. You'll be spoilt for choice in this 19th-century palace turned hotel: enjoy a caviar facial, a chocolate body pack, a hot stone treatment or a relaxing Ayurveda massage? A fabulous view of the gardens surrounding the palace is included – giving the eyes a treat, too *(Rua Jau 54* **(128 A4)** *(*∅ *F10)* | tel. 2 13 61 56 00 | www.pestana.com | best* take a taxi)*. For complete relaxation, take an hour in the saline solution of the ● *Float In* floating tank. The brain switches off completely, and the leg muscles can unwind from a day spent pounding the city streets *(40 min. from 30 euros)*. Extensive selection of massages *(Rua de S. Filipe Nery 37 A* **(130 A2)** *(*∅ *K8)* | tel. 2 13 88 01 93 or 9 15 78 58 21 | www.float-in.pt | Metro (yellow) Rato).*

taken alongside the statue have actually read Pessoa's obsessive prose and poetry, tinged with nihilism. Pessoa's name and his work are intimately connected with the city. As witty as he was eccentric, the intellectual wrote under different names – 'heteronyms', whose identity he would take on for a certain time – worked as a foreign languages correspondence clerk in the Baixa and moved house many times within the city. During his lifetime, Pessoa, whose name means 'person', published very little, but his work is currently experiencing a renaissance beyond the borders of Portugal. In the poet's last residence, which has been converted into a small arts centre with a library, fans can follow in the footsteps of this genius of modernism *(Casa Fernando Pessoa | Rua Coelho da Rocha 16 | Mon–Sat 10am–6pm | free admission | casafernandopessoa.cm-lisboa.pt, mundopessoa.blogs.sapo.pt | Eléctrico 25, 28 to Rua Saraiva Carvalho)*. Still worth reading: Pessoa's poetic city guide written in 1930, Lisbon – what the Tourist Should See.

SAUDADE

'Like a dagger working in the heart' is how the Portuguese will sometimes explain the feeling of sheer boundless melancholy known as *saudade* – a word that cannot be translated as sorrow, fatalism, sentimentalism, nostalgia or melancholy, as it combines a little bit of all of them. The roots of this passionate feeling are considered to lie in the Islamic era, and it finds its artistic expression in the famous fado music. In conversation with Lisbon's older generation, you'll often find a general fatalism at work. When asked how things are going, they will often reply, 'Eh, cá estou' (well, here I am) or 'Vai-se andando' (things are going), comparable perhaps to the English expression 'mustn't grumble'.

São Vicente, Lisbon's official patron saint

THE PERFECT DAY
Lisbon in 24 hours

08:00am AFTER BREAKFAST: DOWN TO THE RIVER

There are, of course, many different ways of having a perfect day in Lisbon. In any case, for lisboetas, a day usually begins with a good *cafézinho* – for instance in the historic *Café Nicola (Rua 1° de Dezembro 20)* right on central *Rossio → p. 39* (photo top left). Take a leisurely stroll down the main shopping street, *Rua Augusta*, in the direction of the Tagus. You are in the heart of downtown, the Baixa, which was laid out in a spacious grid design after the devastating earthquake of 1755.

09:00am GO WITH THE FLOW

An imposing triumphal arch leads you on to the *Praça do Comércio → p. 37*, aka *Terreiro do Paço* (Square of the Palace). The palace was entirely destroyed by the 1755 earthquake; luckily, the royal family was elsewhere at the time. Here, a grand view of the Tagus opens up. An extensive clean-up of the river in 2011, and new restaurants and cafés, have greatly enhanced the square, with its fine arcade of yellow-painted buildings. At its centre, an equestrian statue of King José I symbolically tramples serpents underfoot; it was created in 1775 by Machado de Castro, the top sculptor of the period.

10:00am BY TRAM THROUGH THE ALFAMA

Now turn away from the river, towards Rossio again, and board the famous Eléctrico No. 28 in Rua Conceição (making sure your wallet is safely stowed away). Ride for a few stops aboard this picturesque yellow tram, through Lisbon's labyrinthine Old Town – past the *Sé Cathedral → p. 32* – up into the attractive quarter of *Alfama → p. 28*. Get off at the Largo Portas do Sol, where the terrace-café *Esplanada das Portas do Sol* offers a fabulous view of the Alfama rooftops and the Tagus. Take a break and stop for a cool drink before continuing on foot. From here, it is only a short, if fairly steep, walk up to the castle. Take the steps at the Largo behind you and follow the picturesquely dilapidated Rua dos Cegos around to the left, then take a right into Rua Santa Cruz do Castelo.

Get to know some of the most dazzling, exciting, and relaxing facets of Lisbon – all on a single day

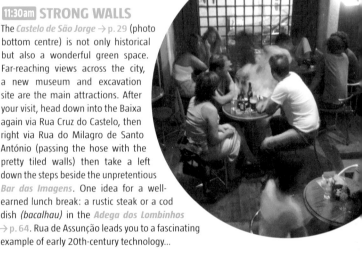

11:30am STRONG WALLS

The *Castelo de São Jorge* → p. 29 (photo bottom centre) is not only historical but also a wonderful green space. Far-reaching views across the city, a new museum and excavation site are the main attractions. After your visit, head down into the Baixa again via Rua Cruz do Castelo, then right via Rua do Milagro de Santo António (passing the hose with the pretty tiled walls) then take a left down the steps beside the unpretentious *Bar das Imagens*. One idea for a well-earned lunch break: a rustic steak or a cod dish *(bacalhau)* in the *Adega dos Lombinhos* → p. 64. Rua de Assunção leads you to a fascinating example of early 20th-century technology...

02:30pm UPLIFTING SHOPPING

No, it wasn't Gustave Eiffel himself who designed the *Elevador de Santa Justa* → p. 35, but a pupil of his. No matter, the cast-iron structure, completed in 1901, is still fabulous. If the queue for the tickets appears too long for comfort, climb the steps and head left on Rua do Carmo into well-heeled *Chiado* → p. 39 with its chic shops. Art lovers can get a quick overview of modern Portuguese art at the *Museo do Chiado* → p. 42.

07:30pm OPEN END

Time for dinner? The fancy tasting menu at *100 Maneiras* → p. 61 is meant to be savoured. Afterwards, just around the corner, the traditional port wine institute *Solar do Vinho do Porto* → p. 42 is a good choice for a relaxing digestif before hitting the city's nightlife. In the entertainment quarter of *Bairro Alto* → p. 39 (photo top right), the party starts late – 11pm at the earliest. Here's a tip to avoid hanging onto your Caipiroska straw on your own: while you're waiting, explore the original shops of the bairro, get a trendy haircut, or use the time to purchase some attractive souvenirs from *Cork & Co* → p. 69. Boa noite!

Metro to the starting point: green
Stop: Rossio
Eléctrico: line no. 28

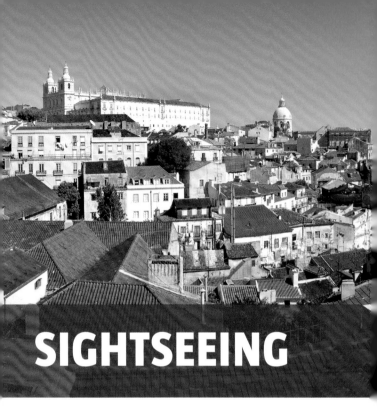

SIGHTSEEING

CITY **WHERE TO START?**
Rossio (131 D4) (∅ M9): From Rossio, officially Praça Dom Pedro IV, either stay on the flat and reach the banks of the Tagus in a 10-min walk or head up the hill to the **Castelo de São Jorge** (approx. 20 min). Or take Rua do Carmo, again uphill, in the direction of **Chiado** for shopping and interesting monuments and museums. The fastest way to get to the party zone of **Bairro Alto** is to head for the **Restauradores** square and take the **Elevador da Glória** funicular from there. The Metro station is Rossio (green); many buses pass the square, including the fast airport service no. 91.

While Lisbon has no shortage of grand monuments, it's most of all the small things that make the city on the Tagus what it is. The best way to explore and experience the capital is on foot.

Stroll across magnificent squares, lose yourself in the maze of alleyways, and enjoy fantastic views from the many *miradouros* (viewpoints) of the city built on seven hills. Join the lisboetas in one of the many Lisbon cafés for a *bica* (espresso) or a *galão* (milky coffee). Or board one of the ancient trams. A ride on the ★ ● *Eléctrico 28* is one of the best and cheapest tours of Lisbon, as it trundles through the entire city centre. In order to get a seat, it's best to board at the beginning of the run, at Martim Moniz, for example. Without wanting

Photo: view across the Old Town neighbourhood of Alfama

A ride on the funicular or a stroll through narrow alleyways – it's the little pleasures that make Lisbon a big adventure

to dampen the holiday spirit: do watch your wallet!

In the light of the setting sun, Lisbon shows off its classic beauty. **INSIDER TIP** The best vantage point for catching this mood is the river. Just board one of the many ● Tagus ferries, and take a little detour to the other side of the river, from central Cais do Sodré to Cacilhas for instance. Close to the ferry port you'll find a couple of **INSIDER TIP** attractive terrace restaurants on the river. The national museums of the capital are dedicated to the glorious past of Portugal. Again and again, the themes revolve around the exciting time of the Discoveries, Portugal's empire and the Golden Age. Works of art and precious artefacts from that era give a glimpse of former prosperity. Exotic treasures from foreign lands are a reminder of the past glories of this small country. Many Lisbon museums are housed in palaces that used to belong to the nobility, making them worth seeing for this reason alone. Even if you can't bear museums,

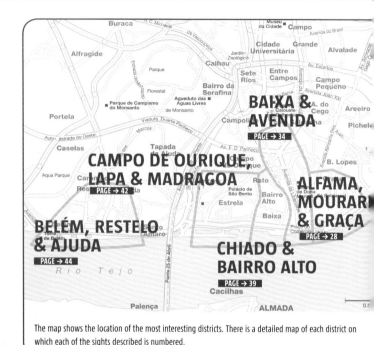

The map shows the location of the most interesting districts. There is a detailed map of each district on which each of the sights described is numbered.

be aware that INSIDER TIP some of the most beautiful terrace cafés belong to museums, the garden café of the Museu Nacional de Arte Antiga among them.

Those not so fleet of foot, or retro lovers, will appreciate the old-fashioned *elevadores* (lifts) that make short work of some of Lisbon's hills. They include three funiculars – two carriages that pull each other up using a sophisticated pulley system. All of these curious means of transport are over 100 years old. A one-off transport ticket costs 3.50 euros; you're much better off buying an all-day ticket (3.95 euros) for Metro and Carris (the company that runs the buses and *elevadores*).

ALFAMA, MOURARIA & GRAÇA

MAP INSIDE BACK COVER
Old Lisbon clusters around the Castelo de São Jorge, with the historic neighbourhoods of Alfama and Mouraria nestling below.

The former Moorish settlement of Alfama is Lisbon's oldest neighbourhood. Miraculously, the quarter survived the devastating earthquake of 1755 virtually unscathed, and its medieval character has been preserved. This *bairro histórico* is a modest working-class area characterised by a maze of steep, narrow stairs, tiny lanes and leafy squares. Similarly labyrinthine, but more derelict, yet on the rise is neighbouring Mouraria. This is where the Moors were banished after the Christian reconquest of the city in 1147. In June, Alfama celebrates its patron saint, Santo António, with street parties, music and dance. Adjoining Alfama, to the northeast, is Graça, a vibrant 19th-century residential quarter. Graça has several magnificent buildings, including the monastery church of *São Vicente de Fora* and the *Pantheon*, as well as some glorious viewpoints. On Saturdays and Tuesdays, the *Campo de Santa Clara* is the setting for the *Feira da Ladra* flea market.

1 CASA DO FADO/MUSEU DO FADO (131 F5) *(🕮 O9)*

The fado museum offers an entertaining exploration of the history and contemporary role of fado. An audioguide allows visitors to experience the artists and their music, such as INSIDER TIP virtuoso guitarist Carlos Paredes. The museum's chic restaurant puts on evening fado shows, accompanied by modern Portuguese cuisine *(Moderate). Tue–Sun 10am–6pm | admission 3 euros | Largo do Chafariz de Dentro 1 | bus 28 to Casa Conto*

2 CASA DOS BICOS (131 E5) *(🕮 N10)*

The *House of Spikes* owes its name to its façade of pointy stonework. The son of the viceroy of India, Brás de Albuquerque, had this city palace built in Italian style in 1523. Today, the foundation honouring the memory of the late Nobel-Prize winning author José Saramago has its headquarters here. Saramago's ashes were buried on the small lawn in front of the building. *Rua dos Bacalhoeiros | eléctrico 18, 25 to Rua Alfândega*

3 CASTELO DE SÃO JORGE ★ (131 E4) *(🕮 N9)*

The castle dedicated to St George is the

MARCO POLO HIGHLIGHTS

★ Eléctrico 28
Trundle through the entire city centre aboard the famous tram → p. 26

★ Castelo de São Jorge
The medieval castle above Alfama marks the nucleus of Lisbon's urban development → p. 29

★ Rossio
This bustling, urban heart of the capital has a beautiful railway station (trains to Sintra), theatres, a church and cafés → p. 39

★ Igreja São Roque
The austere façade conceals a splendid chapel, its most beautiful altar freshly restored → p. 41

★ Mosteiro dos Jerónimos
An empire turned to stone: the pièce de résistance of Manueline style → p. 45

★ Museu de Marinha
Testimonies from Portugal's Age of Discovery → p. 46

★ Torre de Belém
A symbol of the city for the last 500 years → p. 50

★ Museu de Calouste Gulbenkian
This welcoming and varied museum shelters incredible treasures → p. 51

★ Museu Nacional do Azulejo
Find out everything about Portuguese tile art → p. 52

★ Parque das Nações
Avant-garde architecture plus a stat-of-the-art aquarium → p. 53

of Lisbon. Impossible to miss, it occupies a prominent position above the rooftops of the city. The steep climb up the castle hill is rewarded by amazing views. ● You can recuperate from your exertions on the stone benches under shady trees. This medieval citadel was a base for many of the country's rulers, as the difficult-to-capture castle hill gave a wide-ranging view of the entire city and the Tagus delta. Founded in the fifth century by the Visigoths, the fort was taken and extended by the Moors in 716. In 1147, King Dom Afonso Henriques and his followers, aided by Crusaders from England recaptured the castle. Turned into a royal residence, it underwent many alterations and extensions over the following centuries. In the early 16th century, the Portuguese royal family (King Manuel I) moved to a new palace of the edge of the Tagus, and the castle was left to fall into disrepair. To mark the 800th anniversary of the *Reconquista* (reconquest), the fort and its defensive towers were reconstructed into a Salazarist-style fantasy of what a castle should look like.

A well-displayed exhibition showing archaeological finds dating back to the Iron Age documents the way of life and customs of the former inhabitants of the castle mound. On the *Ulisses* Tower, the periscope of the *Câmara Escura* (camera obscura) projects a 360-degree panorama of the city onto a stone bowl, and a **INSIDER TIP** brand-new multimedia show tells the story of Lisbon. *Castle compound: daily, Nov–Feb 9am–6pm, March–Oct 9am–9pm | admission 7 euros incl. museum, Câmara Escura (9am–5pm) and multimedia show | www.castelode saojorge.pt | eléctrico 12, 28 to Miradouro de Santa Luzia, bus 37 to Castelo*

Today, the Igreja de Santa Engrácia serves as Portugal's national pantheon

■4■ IGREJA E CONVENTO DA GRAÇA
(131 E3) (∅ N8)

The 13th-century three-naved Augustine convent that originally stood on this spot was damaged to such an extent by the earthquake in 1755 that the building was completely rebuilt, this time with only one nave. Since 1834, the main convent buildings have been occupied by the military and are not open to the public. However, the church is usually open. In front of it is the delightful and well-known viewpoint *Miradouro da Graça* and café with table service. *Eléctrico 28 to Graça*

5 IGREJA DE SANTA ENGRÁCIA / PANTEÃO NACIONAL ⚜

(131 F4) (∅ O9)

The tall white dome of this church, a national pantheon for the great and the good of the city, can be seen from afar. The first woman to be buried here was fado queen Amália Rodrigues whose sarcophagus was interred here in 2001,

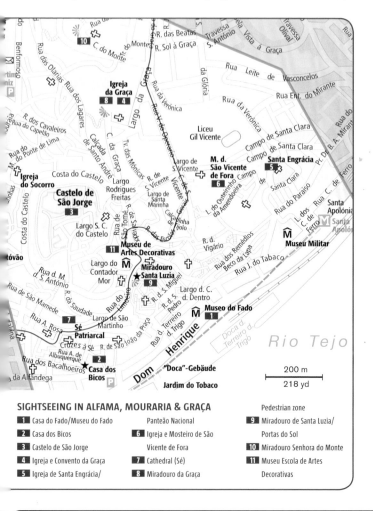

SIGHTSEEING IN ALFAMA, MOURARIA & GRAÇA

1 Casa do Fado/Museu do Fado
2 Casa dos Bicos
3 Castelo de São Jorge
4 Igreja e Convento da Graça
5 Igreja de Santa Engrácia/

Panteão Nacional
6 Igreja e Mosteiro de São
Vicente de Fora
7 Cathedral (Sé)
8 Miradouro da Graça

Pedestrian zone

9 Miradouro de Santa Luzia/
Portas do Sol
10 Miradouro Senhora do Monte
11 Museu Escola de Artes
Decorativas

transferred from its original burial place. The history of the church explains the popular expression of *obras de Santa Engrácia* for ventures that seem to take forever: the first foundations were laid in 1570; of that structure nothing has been preserved. On 15 January 1630, the vestry and paintings inside the church were destroyed. A young man called Simão Pires Sólis was accused of the crime, and prophesied on the way to the scaffold that the church would never be finished. In fact, the church was eventually dedicated in 1966 – some 400 years after work started.

It is worth exploring the interior to appreciate the harmonious colours and shapes of this well-proportioned building. A lift takes visitors up to the terrace around the mighty dome, affording INSIDER TIP amazing views on all sides. On Tuesdays and Saturdays, the *Feira da Ladra* flea market takes place on the Campo de Santa Clara – another good reason to come here. *Tue–Sun 10am–5pm | admission 3 euros (Sun free until 2pm) | Campo de Santa Clara | eléctrico 28 to Voz Operário*

▮6▮ IGREJA E MOSTEIRO DE SÃO VICENTE DE FORA ↘↙
(131 F4) (⌂ O9)

This bright white Renaissance building marks a towering presence in Graça. King Philip II of Spain (Dom Filipe I of Portugal) commissioned the monastery in 1582, and work continued up until the early 18th century. Inside, you'll find marble splendour, choir stalls made from tropical hardwood and blue-and-white azulejos, decorating the cloisters. Today the monastery is the headquarters of the cardinal *(patriarca)* of Lisbon, as well as serving as the burial place for the kings of the Bragança dynasty. The peace of the place is enhanced by beautiful views

across the city. *Tue–Sun 10am–5pm | admission 4 euros | Largo de São Vicente | eléctrico 28 to Voz Operário*

▮7▮ CATHEDRAL (SÉ) (131 E5) (⌂ N9)

The cathedral or Sé (short for *sedes episcopalism*, bishopric in English) is the oldest church in Lisbon. Built after the Moors were driven out of the city in 1147, it is said to have replaced a five-naved mosque. The cathedral was damaged by various earthquakes, and restored several times over at the beginning of the 20th century. Today, it combines two architectural styles, apparent in the sober Romanesque interior and the elegant Gothic cloisters with nine chapels. In the garden of the 14th-century Gothic cloisters, archaeological excavations have been going on for years, revealing Roman traces, including the remains of a street and canalisation systems, dating back to the first century. Few visitors

bother with the treasury, reached by the stairs immediately right after the entrance, but the church treasure – relics, and a superb golden monstrance (1760) – are worth taking in. *Church daily 9am–7pm, cloisters and chapels daily 10am–6pm | admission 2.50 euros | treasury Mon–Fri 10am–1pm, 2–5pm, Sat 10am–5pm | admission 2.50 euros, Mass: Sun/holidays 11.30am and 7pm, Tue–Sat 6.30pm | Largo da Sé | eléctrico 28, bus 37 to Sé*

8 MIRADOURO DA GRAÇA ☼
(131 E3) (⌘ N8)

A few trees, a few tables and chairs and a small café-kiosk make this a favourite meeting place for a sundowner. There are fabulous views across to the castle and the magnificent Baixa all the way to the 25 April bridge. *Eléctrico 28 to Largo da Graça*

9 MIRADOURO DE SANTA LUZIA/PORTAS DO SOL ☼
(131 E5) (⌘ N9)

This viewing terrace offers fine views across the dense sea of rooftops and the maze of alleys that makes up Alfama, as well as across the Tagus. The azulejo wall on the *Santa Luzia* church portrays Lisbon before the fateful earthquake of 1755. A little further up, on the *Largo das Portas do Sol* you'll find a small café kiosk, and just around the corner the chic ● *Esplanada das Portas do Sol. Eléctrico 12 and 28 to Miradouro de Santa Luzia*

10 MIRADOURO SENHORA DO MONTE ☼ (131 E3) (⌘ N8)

See Lisbon and the Tagus spread out below you from the highest *miradouro* in town. This calm and picturesque little space seems far removed from the hustle and bustle of the big city. There is a statue of the Virgin Mary and a small

Superb view across Alfama's sea of roofs from the Mirador de Santa Luzia

pilgrimage chapel, containing, behind a locked door (asked to be shown) the 12th-century seat of St Gens, traditionally used by women hoping to conceive. *Eléctrico 28 to Rua da Graça*

⓫ MUSEU ESCOLA DE ARTES DECORATIVAS ⚘ (131 E4) *(⏉ N9)*

The Espírito Santo family – one of the richest in Portugal – has donated furniture and other precious items to this museum. Alongside furniture, the museum for applied arts, housed in the noble 17th-century *Palácio Azurara*, shows tapestries and carpets, azulejos, china and silver. Nearby, you'll find three *miradouros (see above)*. *Wed–Mon 10am–5pm | admission 4 euros | Largo das Portas do Sol 2 | www.fress. pt | eléctrico 28 to Largo das Portas do Sol*

BAIXA & AVENIDA

The Baixa (Downtown) stretches from splendid Praça do Comércio on the banks of the Tagus to busy Rossio.

The broad pedestrian zone of Rua Augusta represents the main artery of this traditional business and banking quarter. The district was formed following the 1755 earthquake as a quarter for artisans. The foreign minister of the time, Marquês de Pombal, had it laid out in a grid. Today, the street names are a reminder of the Marquês's plan to allocate one street to each craft guild. *Rua dos Sapateiros* (Street of the Shoemakers)

EAGLES OR LIONS

● A true lisboeta, they say, has to nail their colours to the mast: either red for the Eagles *(Águias)* of Benfica or green for the Lions *(Leões)* of Sporting, the two clubs that, along with Porto in the north of Portugal, dominate Portuguese football. In 2006, Benfica had its Guinness Book of Records status confirmed as the football club with most registered members. For over 100 years, the cult around the two traditional clubs has divided the capital's football fans. Their stadiums, which are less than 3km (1.5 mi) apart, were both built from scratch for the European Championships in 2004. Benfica's *Estádio da Luz* (Stadium of Light) **(118 B3) *(⏉ O)*** holds about 65,000 spectators, Sporting's *Estádio José Alvalade* **(119 F1) *(⏉ O)*** holds 52,000. On match days, fans from half the country descend on Lisbon hours

before kick-off, and the powerful fan clubs get things going with plenty of noise, flag waving and banners. Tickets for league games cost 5–35 euros; order at the stadium ticket desks or online *(Mon–Fri 10am–7pm | pick-up 2 hrs before kick-off at the latest | www. slbenfica.pt and www.sporting.pt)*. Both stadiums can be visited, with Alvalade also boasting the *Mundo Sporting* museum, an educational monument to the club's glory. *Estádio José Alvalade | daily 11am–6pm, on match days only up to 3/4pm | admission 8 euros | ticket desk Hall VIP 12.30–7.30pm on the day before and on match days from 9am | Metro (yellow) Campo Grande; Estádio da Luz | daily except match days | admission 10 euros | ticket desk Door/Porta 18 | 9.30am–12.30pm, 2–5.30pm | Metro (blue) Colégio Militar/Luz*

is worth a detour to visit *A Camponesa*, a wonderfully old-fashioned café, while *Fragoleto* in *Rua da Prata 74* (Street of Silver) serves excellent takeaway ice cream with unusual flavours – try the carob and basil. To the north, the magnificent boulevard *Avenida da Liberdade* leads up to the square dedicated to the great urban innovator, *Praça Marquês de Pombal*. A particularly fine view of the boulevard can be enjoyed from the top-class restaurant *Terraço* on the ninth floor of the luxury Tivoli hotel.

■1 AVENIDA DA LIBERDADE

(130 B2/C3) (Ⓜ L7–8, M8)

This splendid boulevard forms the bridge between the old and the new Lisboa. At around 1.5km (1mi), the Avenida was laid out in 1886 to connect the Praça dos Restauradores with the Praça Marquês de Pombal. Tree-lined strips of lawn with cafés separate the street from the mosaic-adorned pavements. The boulevard is lined with elegant hotels, boutiques and fancy townhouses, but also has a few eyesores and the odd façade with none-too attractive graffiti. Pretty and stylish: the INSIDER **TIP** Tea Room of Portuguese fashion brand *Lanidor (Hausnr. 1772)*. 2011 saw a revitalisation of the Avenida, with new kiosks and bars. *Metro (blue) Restauradores, Avenida, Marquês de Pombal*

■2 ELEVADOR DA GLÓRIA

(130 C4) (Ⓜ M9)

The most central and popular *elevador* has been connecting downtown Baixa with party-central Bairro Alto since 1885, which is why it operates up to midnight during the week and until 4.30am at weekends. The 'valley station' lies on *Praça dos Restauradores* near the tourist information, the 'hill station' next to the pretty viewpoint *Miradouro São Pedro de Alcântara*. *Metro (blue) Restauradores*

The Elevador da Lavra has been working for nearly 130 years

■3 ELEVADOR DA LAVRA

(130 C3) (Ⓜ M8)

This is the city's oldest *elevador*, dating from 1884. It takes people up to one of most secluded and least touristy viewpoints in Lisbon, the Jardim de Torel. *Mon–Sat 7am–9pm, Sun 9am–9pm | Metro (blue) Restauradores*

■4 ELEVADOR DE SANTA JUSTA ● ⋇

(131 D4–5) (Ⓜ M9)

The undisputed star among Lisbon's *elevadores*, this cast-iron construction is a proper lift. Its spacious wooden cars are pulled up to a height of 30m (100ft). Also called Elevador do Carmo, it was built by Raul Mesnier de Ponsard, a pupil of Gustave Eiffel's. The elevator was inaugurated in 1902. At the top you'll find a viewing terrace and the passage onto the Bairro Alto, with a recent addition: the Italian restaurant ✂ *Bella Lisa Elevador (www.bellalisaelevador.com | Moderate)*, which offers a lunchtime pasta buffet. *Daily 9am–11pm, in winter to 9pm | Metro (blue, green) Baixa-Chiado*

5 JARDÍM BOTÂNICO (130 B3) (*ω L8*)
This green, if slightly neglected-looking, oasis is ideal for a little stroll or just

Elevador de Santa Justa also has a viewing terrace

some respite from the city bustle. The ancient tropical trees of the garden, which were laid out in 1873, are mainly from the former Portuguese colonies. Ponds, elegant stairways and statues lend the park a charming-picturesque look. *Daily 10am–8pm, in winter 10am–6pm | admission 1.50 euros | Rua da Escola Politécnica 58 | Metro (yellow) Rato*

6 MUDE (131 D5) (*ω M10*)
The Museum for Design and Fashion (*mude* meaning both 'it is changing' or 'change!') is housed in a former bank and presents its permanent exhibition of iconic fashion and furniture in a postmodern, industrial ambience; changing exhibitions and installations are staged on the second and third floors. *Tue–Thu, Sun 10am–8pm, Fri/Sat to 10pm | admission (still) free | Rua Augusta 24 | Metro (blue) Terreiro do Paço*

7 PARQUE EDUARDO VII ✂
(130 A–B1) (*ω K–L 6–7*)
Long rather than wide, this park extends up the hill behind the Marquês de Pombal square. Fine vistas are to be had from the upper end of the park. On a fine day, the view extends almost to the other shore of the Tagus. Few tourists find their way into the INSIDER TIP ▶ *Estufas* (hothouses) at the top end of the park, but they are real gems and well worth seeking out. Established in the early 20th century, the contain plants from all over the world. The wooden slats on the roof of the *Estufa fria* helps shelter the plants from the heat of the sun – hence 'cold' hothouse – while cacti and other tropical plants thrive in the adjacent *Estufa quente* ('hot' hothouse). *Daily 9am–6pm or 9am–5pm (winter) | admission 1.65 euros | Metro (blue) Marquês de Pombal, Parque, S. Sebastião*

8 PRAÇA DO COMÉRCIO (TERREIRO DO PAÇO) (131 D5–6) (*M–N10*)
Among Lisbon's many squares, the *Trade Square* takes pride of place. Flanked by beautiful yellow buildings with arcaded walkways on three sides, the generously laid out square opens out towards the Tagus. Unsurprisingly, this was the location of the royal residence before the earthquake of 1755, hence the still-used name (also the Metro stop) *Terreiro do Paço* (Palace Square). In the centre of the square stands the equestrian statue of King José I, the monarch who commissioned Marquês de Pombal to rebuild the city. In 2011, the square was given a makeover. A new complex, the *Patio da Galé*, brings together a tourist informa-

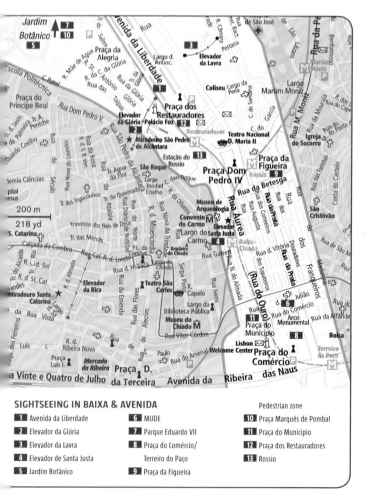

On his high horse – King José I dominates the Praça do Comércio

tion, café and ice cream parlour, the well-stocked *Lisboa Shop* and the *Terreiro do Paço* gourmet restaurant. *Metro (blue) Terreiro do Paço*

⑨ PRAÇA DA FIGUEIRA
(131 D4) (*M9*)
Only a row of houses separates this square from its more glamorous cousin Rossio (see below). Its hallmarks are the pigeons fluttering around the equestrian statue of King João I and the young skateboarders. *Metro (green) Rossio*

⑩ PRAÇA MARQUÊS DE POMBAL
(130 B1–2) (*L7*)
This rounded square marks the border between old and new Lisbon. Amid the chaotic traffic, a statue of man responsible for urban renewal following the 1755 earthquake, Marquês de Pombal, looks down onto his life's work. *Metro (blue, yellow) Marquês de Pombal*

⑪ PRAÇA DO MUNICIPIO
(131 D5) (*M10*)
This is the city hall (*Câmara Municipal*), the historical stage for the proclamation of the Republic in 1910. The neoclassical building is open to visitors on Sundays at 11am. The twisted double column on the square once served as the local pillory. *Eléctrico 15, 18 to Praça do Comércio, Metro (green, blue) Baixa-Chiado*

⑫ PRAÇA DOS RESTAURADORES
(130 C3–4) (*M8–9*)
In the centre of the square, a soaring 30m-high (100ft) obelisk commemorates the liberation of Portugal from the Spanish yoke in 1640. Today, the day of Victory in the War of Restoration is a national holiday (1 December). Recent suggestions to do away with this public holiday in order to help address the deficit were met with howls of protest. Once home to dictator Salazar's propaganda

machine, *Palácio Foz* on the edge of the square today welcomes visitors with a tourist information post and the tourist police. *Metro (blue) Restauradores*

13 ROSSIO ⭐ (131 D4) *(𝓜 M9)*
Hear the heartbeat of the city in this popular square, which is always thronged with people and full of life. The square, which is paved in an ● artistic wave mosaic, is flanked by the long-established cafés *Suiça* (sometimes with nerve-racking 'free' entertainment outside) and *Nicola*. The northern side is occupied by the neoclassical national theatre *Dona Maria II*. To the right, set a little bit back from the square, stands the *Igreja São Domingos,* where the Inquisition once sat in judgement. A stone monument in front of the church commemorates the 1506 pogrom against the Jews, which started here. Cross the road for the neo-Manueline Rossio Train Station, with its pretty horse-shoe shaped entrances and one of the few *Starbucks* in town. Around Rossio, several tiny bars vie to serve the INSIDER **TIP** *Ginginja* cherry liqueur, whose popularity transcends generations and social class. *Metro (green) Rossio*

CHIADO & BAIRRO ALTO

While Chiado proper covers just a few streets, much of the city's soul resides here.

For centuries, the 'Meridian of the literati', as the late Lisbon author José Cardoso Pires called it, was the meeting point for artists, poets and intellectuals. Here you'll find Portugal's most famous literary figure Fernando Pessoa in front

BOOKS & FILMS

▶ **Lisbon Requiem** – The late great Lusophile Italian Antonio Tabucchi describes a 'dream day' in the blazingly hot city

▶ **Lisbon Logbook** – Witty, charming and with an expert's eye, the late José Cardoso Pires describes the city, its inhabitants and their idiosyncratic ways in short essays

▶ **Pereira Maintains** – Tabucchi's sensitive novel on a process of political awakening, set in Lisbon in 1938, was made into a film in 1996, starring Marcello Mastroianni

▶ **Lisbon Story** – Acclaimed filmmaker Wim Wenders, an avowed Lisbon fan, made this film about making a film in Lisbon in 1994. Atmospheric backdrops and the fitting music by Portuguese band Madredeus make this movie well worth seeing

▶ **April Captains** – The Portuguese actress Maria de Medeiros directed this film (made in 2000) about the events of the Carnation Revolution on 25 April 1974

▶ **Taxi Lisboa** – In this 1996 film, documentary maker Wolf Gaudlitz captured a fine portrait of the oldest taxi driver in Lisbon, the late Augusto Macedo, plying the streets of the Portuguese capital aboard his Oldsmobile

of his favourite café, *A Brasileira*, as well as the *São Carlos* opera, several splendid theatres and the best antiques shops in town. When, in August 1988, a major

Chiado. Dating from 1892, its short track is so narrow in places that you can practically peer through the windows of the houses and see what people are cook-

Rack and ruin: only a few elegant columns are left of the Igreja do Carmo

fire destroyed a large chunk of Chiado, the whole of Lisbon was under shock for days. Now most of the damage has been repaired and the area is as it was before, an elegant shopping mile pulsating with life. The adjacent Bairro Alto quarter is Lisbon's traditional party zone. It played an important role in the 1980s for young lisboetas shaking off the years of dictatorship. Alongside pubs, restaurants, bars and clubs, one-off shops with long opening hours ensure a steady flow of visitors. In the morning, when the detritus of the night before has been cleared away, the small Old Town quarter shows a very different face of pleasant peace and calm.

■ ELEVADOR DA BICA
(130 B–C5) (*M L9–10*)
The smallest *elevador* leads up from Rua da Boavista to Calçada do Combro near

ing for dinner. *Mon–Sat 7am–9pm, Sun 9am–9pm | Metro (green) Cais do Sodré or (green, blue) Baixa-Chiado*

2 IGREJA DO CARMO
(130 C4–5) (*M M9*)
Visible from afar, the ruined Carmo church rises high above the Old Town as a stone memento mori. The great Gothic 14th-century convent was all but destroyed by the 1755 earthquake. All that remained standing were a few elegant columns and arches. Occasional open-air classical concerts take place inside the roofless nave. The lateral wings house a fascinating archaeological museum. The church lies on leafy Largo do Carmo with a small playful fountain and a café. *Mon–Sat 10am–6pm, Oct–April only to 5pm | admission 2.50 euros | Largo do Carmo | Metro (blue, green) Baixa-Chiado*

▣ IGREJA SÃO ROQUE ★
(130 C4) (*ঞ M9*)

The simple façade of the church doesn't suggest the glorious splendour inside. Built in 1566, the Jesuit church survived the 1755 earthquake nearly undamaged. The most splendid of the eight lateral chapels is the one dedicated to John the Baptist *(Capela de São João Baptista)* on the left, near the altar. King João V commissioned it in 1742 from Rome. With money no object, the best artists were commissioned and only the most precious materials used – Carrara marble, ivory, gold, silver and precious stones. After being blessed by the Pope, the chapel was shipped to Lisbon in individual parts to be rebuilt in situ. In 2012, the chapel reopened to visitors after extensive restoration works. The *Museu de São Roque* boasts the second-largest collection of relics after the Escorial in Madrid. *Church Mon 2–6pm, Tue–Sun 9am–6pm, Thu to 9pm | free admission | museum closed Mon, Thu 2–9pm, other days 10am–6pm | admission 2.50 euros (● Sun until 2pm free admission) | Sun 3pm free guided tour | Largo Trindade Coelho | Metro (blue) Baixa-Chiado or Restauradores, then Elevador da Glória; eléctrico 28 to Largo do Camões*

▣ INSIDER TIP ▶ MIRADOURO DE SANTA CATARINA ঌ৺
(130 B5) (*ঞ L10*)

This square, with its far-reaching views across the port and the Tagus towards

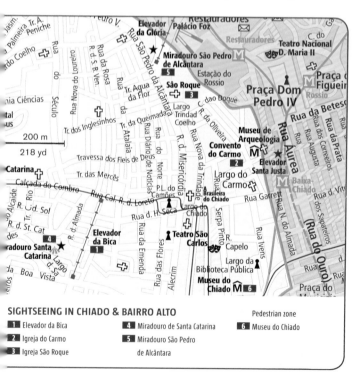

SIGHTSEEING IN CHIADO & BAIRRO ALTO

Pedestrian zone

▣ Elevador da Bica
▣ Igreja do Carmo
▣ Igreja São Roque

▣ Miradouro de Santa Catarina
▣ Miradouro São Pedro
   de Alcântara

▣ Museu do Chiado

the Atlantic, was made for balmy summer nights. Below the small café kiosk, open daily from noon onwards (weather permitting) is a meeting point for a youthful alternative scene. The evenings have a party feel, with a subtle waft of hash. A more upmarket alternative is the beautiful terrace of the trendy yet child-friendly (play corner with toys!) *noobai* café/bar next door. *Eléctrico 28 to Calhariz-Bica*

⑤ MIRADOURO SÃO PEDRO DE ALCÂNTARA ● ⚹⚹
(130 C4) (𝄞 L–M9)

Wooden benches under shady trees, a gently bubbling fountain, and maybe some refreshments from the kiosk – this is a good place to take a break from sightseeing and soak up the atmosphere of Lisbon. The monument depicts newspaper founder Eduardo Coelho and a bronze *ardina*, a typical 19th-century newspaper

boy. Fabulous views take in Old Lisbon with Mouraria and Alfama, the church towers and domes and the Castelo de São Jorge. There is also a simple open-air café. Tucked away behind the *miradouro*, discover the genteel port wine-tasting parlour *Solar do Vinho do Porto*. *Metro (blue) Restauradores, then Elevador da Glória*

⑥ MUSEU DO CHIADO (130 C5) (𝄞 M10)

Lisbon's second museum for contemporary art is housed in the restored *Convento de S. Francisco*. A permanent collection of Portuguese art from the mid-19th century onwards is supplemented by excellent changing exhibitions of modern art and photography. There is also a pretty terrace café. *Tue–Sun 10am–6pm | admission 4 euros | Rua Serpa Pinto 4 | www.museudochiado-ipmuseus.pt | Metro (blue, green) Baixa-Chiado*

CAMPO DE OURIQUE, LAPA & MADRAGOA

The quiet neighbourhood of Campo de Ourique emerged in the late 19th century. Pretty Art Nouveau façades, welcoming cafés and pretty shops are what make this mainly residential quarter so charming.

Lapa, near the Basílica da Estrela, is Lisbon's most well-heeled neighbourhood and the main embassy quarter. The adjoining small district of Madragoa – with its secluded alleyways, little old churches and idyllic small squares – is one of Lisbon's nicest Old Town quarters and also has many sights. The INSIDER TIP eléctrico 25 trundles through these quarters

Right by the park: the Basílica da Estrela

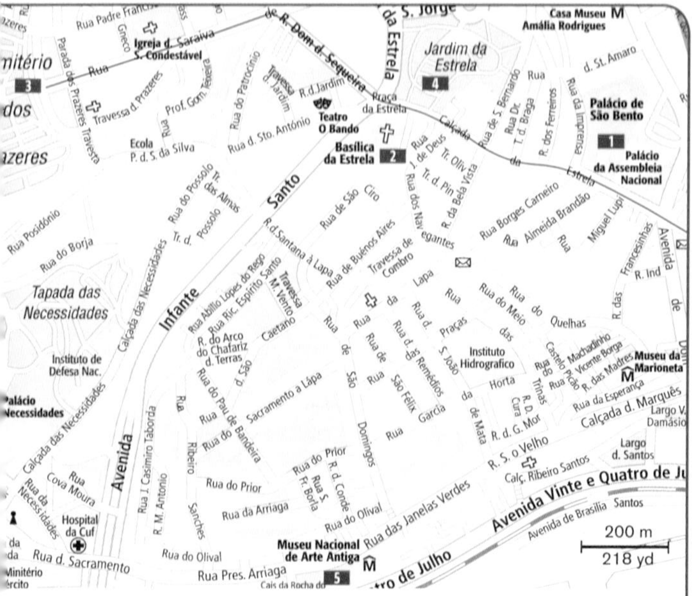

SIGHTSEEING IN CAMPO DE OURIQUE, LAPA & MADRAGOA

1 Assembleia da República/ Palácio de São Bento
2 Basílica da Estrela
3 Cemitério dos Prazeres
4 Jardim da Estrela/Jardim Guerra Junqueiro
Pedestrian zone
5 Museu Nacional de Arte Antiga

1 ASSEMBLEIA DA REPÚBLICA (PALÁCIO DE SÃO BENTO)

(129 F2–3) (*K9*)

This imposing white building is where the Portuguese parliament sits when it is in session. The building was constructed in the 19th century on the ruins of the Benedictine monastery of São Bento de Saúde, whose origins can be traced back to 1598. A wide free-standing staircase, flanked by marble lions, leads up to the main entrance, which is fronted by an impressive set of neoclassical columns. The Prime Minister's offices are to the rear. *Avda. Dom Carlos | www.parlamento.pt | Eléctrico 28 to Calçada Estrela*

2 BASÍLICA DA ESTRELA

(129 E2) (*J9*)

The white dome of the 'Basilica of the Star' stands out on Lisbon's skyline. Visitors can go up into the dome, to enjoy great panoramic views *(admission to the dome 5 euros)*. The funds for building the basilica in 1777 came from Queen Maria I (1734–1816) in gratitude for the birth of a male heir to the throne. Today, it is much in demand for the funerals of the rich and famous. Particularly beautiful is the neoclassical main façade with marble statues *(daily 7.30am–1pm, 5–7pm)*. Don't miss the fabulous ● cork nativity scene towards the back. The city park *Jardim da Estrela* opposite is a good place to relax after visiting. *Eléctrico 28 to Estrela*

■3 CEMITÉRIO DOS PRAZERES
(128 C2–3) (𝕄 H9)

The huge *Cemetery of the Pleasures*, laid out in 1833, is a small city in itself. In death, magnificent mausoleums and modest graves rub shoulders. Many famous Portuguese found their last place of rest here, including Alfredo Keil, composer of the Portuguese national anthem. Poet Fernando Pessoa was originally also laid to rest here, before being transferred to the Hieronymus Monastery. *Oct–April daily 9am–5pm, May–Sept 9am–6pm | Parada dos Prazeres | terminus eléctrico 28*

■4 JARDIM DA ESTRELA
(JARDIM GUERRA JUNQUEIRO)
(129 E3) (𝕄 J–K9)

With its many varied ancient trees, wooden benches under plane trees, a small terrace café and a couple of ponds with ducks and swans, the small urban park in front of the *Basílica da Estrela* is a lovely spot to while away time. At its centre stands a filigree Art Nouveau music pavilion. Tip for families:

a stone's throw away is the excellent ice cream parlour *Artisani* in Avenida Alvares Cabral *(direction of Rato | www.artisani gelado.com)*, which has three swing seats. *Largo da Estrela | eléctrico 28 to Estrela*

■5 MUSEU NACIONAL DE ARTE
ANTIGA ☆ (129 E4) (𝕄 J10)

The National Museum of Ancient Art has one of Portugal's most important art collection. It includes furniture, ceramics, glass, sacred art, silver and gold work, as well as Oriental objects in ivory and mother-of-pearl. It also has an exceptional collection of European masters, with works by Dürer, Holbein, Cranach and Velasquez. The most important painting is the six-piece winged altar by the Portuguese Early Renaissance painter Nuno Gonçalves. Yet it's Hieronymus Bosch's powerful triptych The Temptation of Saint Anthony that is considered the highlight of the museum. After viewing the collection, visit the museum's ☆ terrace bar for views across the river and the port. Next door, in the *Jardim 9 de Abril,* you can enjoy even more spectacular views. The panorama-glass bistro/café cocktail bar *Le Chat (tel. 9 17 79 71 55)* is a trendy spot for a sundowner after the museum closes. Tip: a cheese platter for 8 euros to share and a glass of house red. *Museum: Tue 2–6pm, Wed–Sun 10am–1pm, 2–6pm | admission 4 euros | Rua das Janelas Verdes | www.mnarteantiga-ipmu seus.pt | eléctrico 15 to Cais Rocha*

BELÉM, RESTELO & AJUDA

▨▨ MAP INSIDE BACK COVER
▨▨ Belém (Bethlehem), approx. 7km/4mi west of the city centre, is

Stopping for refreshments: street café in historical Belém

an essential excursion for anyone interested in the history and culture of Lisbon. Here, you can discover some of the top sights of the capital, including the Hieronymus Monastery (Mosteiro dos Jerónimos) or the Torre de Belém. The earthquake of 1755, which shocked a generation, spared this part of town. Thus, after the disaster, Belém and the adjacent quarters of Restelo and Ajuda became a sought-after residential quarter for the nobility and other wealthy citizens. This hasn't changed much since. At the heart of Belém, the pink *Palácio de Belém* has been the seat of the Portuguese president since the founding of the Republic in 1910. Until the proclamation of the Republic, the royal family lived not far from here, at the *Palácio Nacional da Ajuda*. The palace, which was never quite completed, is well worth visiting; it adjoins the *Jardim Botânico da Ajuda (www.jardimbotanicodaajuda. com)*, Portugal's oldest botanical gardens.

■1 MOSTEIRO DOS JERÓNIMOS ★
(126 B–C5) *(m C11)*

It was intended that the Hieronymus Monastery would be the first thing those returning to Lisbon by ship would see on their return. The glory of the Golden Age of the Portuguese Discoveries, and the last place of rest for the great and good of the country, since 1983 the monastery has also been a Unesco World Heritage site. King Manuel I, named the Fortunate *(o Venturoso)*, as his mariners brought him back an empire, laid the first stone for the monastery in 1501. Inspired by the stories told by the seafarers, his architects created extravagant ornaments and decorations. Only centuries later would this idiosyncratic architectural style, between Gothic and Renaissance, be given the name 'Manueline'. King Manuel I was not to see the completion of his monastery. After his death in 1521, it took almost another 50 years for the monastery to be finished. The first features to hit the eye are the two ornate portals, masterpieces of

A highlight from Portugal's Golden Era: Mosteiro dos Jerónimos (Hieronymus Monastery)

stonemasonry. Inside the church, six slender and richly decorated pillars, each 25m (82ft) high, turn into palm trees, with a sky of stars and squares. Bellow the gallery, on either side of the entrance you'll see two splendid sarcophagi. The one containing the mortal remains of Vasco da Gama is decorated with caravels, a globe and the Crusader cross; the other, to the right, of national bard Luís de Camões, is decorated with a quill, laurel wreath and lyre. The author of the Portuguese national epic Os Lusíadas doesn't actually lie here, however; he died of the plague in 1580, completely destitute, and was buried in a Lisbon mass grave. The royal sarcophagi stand inside deep niches at the magnificent high altar, carried by marble elephants. The two-level ● cloisters are an architectural fairytale. With their rampant filigree ornamentation, they are considered among the most beautiful in the world – a fitting environment for the tomb of Fernando Pessoa, the great Modernist poet. The refectory next to the cloisters has extremely fine fan vaulting and pretty azulejo panels from the 18th century. *Cloisters: Oct–April Tue–Sun 10am–5.30pm, May–Sept Tue–Sun 10am–6.30pm | admission 7 euros (free Sun until 2pm), church: admission free | Praça do Império | www.mosteirojeroni mos.pt | eléctrico 15, train from Cais do Sodré to Belém*

2 MUSEU DA MARINHA ★
(126 B5) (*ØJ C11–12*)

Fans of model-making will be in paradise at the Maritime Museum, which is filled with model ships from ancient to contemporary: fishing boats, whalers, rowing galleys, frigates, caravels, sailing yachts, cruise liners, warships, oil tankers. The museum is a monument to Portugal's seafaring history, nautical tradition, and the Age of Discoveries. Also on display are maps, nautical instruments and onboard equipment, log books and paintings. Only a few hundred metres away from the museum is the spot where Captain Vasco da Gama put to sea, over 500 years ago. *Summer* *Tue–Sun 10am–6pm, winter Tue–Sun 10am–5pm | admission 4 euros | Praça do Império | museu.marinha.pt | eléctrico 15 to CCB*

◼3 MUSEU NACIONAL DE ARQUEOLOGIA (126 B–C5) (*ᒲ C11*)

One of the most interesting sections of the Archaeological Museum is the treas-

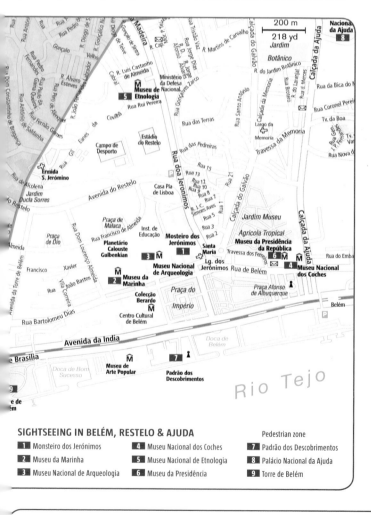

SIGHTSEEING IN BELÉM, RESTELO & AJUDA

Pedestrian zone

- **1** Monsteiro dos Jerónimos
- **2** Museu da Marinha
- **3** Museu Nacional de Arqueologia
- **4** Museu Nacional dos Coches
- **5** Museu Nacional de Etnologia
- **6** Museu da Presidência
- **7** Padrão dos Descobrimentos
- **8** Palácio Nacional da Ajuda
- **9** Torre de Belém

ury. Jewellery and coins from between 20 and 150 AD attest to the rich gold, silver and copper deposits Portugal once had. The mines were exploited to near-exhaustion under the Romans. There are also ancient archaeological finds, artefacts from Egypt, Roman mosaics and medieval tools. Though the museum is housed in the western wing of the *Hieronymus Monastery*, only few tourists find their way here. *Tue–Sun 10am–6pm | admission 4 euros | Praça do Império | www.mnarqueologia-ipmuseus.pt | eléctrico 15 to Monsteiro dos Jerónimos*

16th century in Spain. In late 2013, the collection will move across the road into a new building. At the same time, the Royal Riding School will move back here. Until the opening of the new building, sarcastic graffiti ('Crise?') adorn the temporary curtain wall, questioning whether the money spent on this architecturally ambitious project could have been better spent in these economically austere times. *Tue–Sun 10am–6pm | admission 5 euros | Praça Afonso de Albuquerque | www.museudoscoches.pt | Eléctrico 15 to Belém*

▟ MUSEU NACIONAL DOS COCHES ●
(127 D5) (*ØJ D11*)

The former riding school of the *Palácio de Belém*, today the seat of the Portuguese president, presents a unique collection of coaches and carriages from the 16th to the 19th centuries. Particularly opulent are the triumphal coaches of the Portuguese ambassador to Rome in 1716. The oldest vehicle is also the most modest – the travelling coach of King Philip III (Filipe II of Portugal), built at the end of the

▛ MUSEU NACIONAL DE ETNOLOGIA
(126 B3) (*ØJ C10*)

Delve into foreign cultures in the ethnological museum, which has a comprehensive collection of artefacts from around the world, in particular from Portugal's former colonies. Every six months or so fascinating thematic exhibitions are held. The museum is situated above the Hieronymite Monastery in Belém-Restelo. *Tue 2–6pm, Wed–Sun 10am–6pm | admission 4 euros | Avenida Ilha da Ma*

WILD OR ROMANTIC

Some *lisboetas* prefer the beaches to the west of Lisbon, others swear by the miles of dune-fringed ● *Costa da Caparica*, extending south from the resort of Caparica on the southern shoreline of the Tagus. In summer, a Noddy train runs between the town and the fishing village of Fonte da Telha. Every stop in between has a beach bar; the *Waikiki (stop No. 15 | Praia da Sereia)* is a meeting place for surfers and windsurfers, chic *Borda de Água (No. 14)* is a favourite with the Lisbon jetset, No. 16 has a

kitesurf school with rental *(www.katavento.net)*. Near Sintra, you'll find the extensive sandy beach of *Praia Grande* (with dinosaur footprints above) and the *Praia da Adraga*, between dramatic high rocks. Wild *Praia do Guincho* west of Cascais is a hotspot for all wind and kitesurfers. A semi-nudist beach, and one of the most beautiful in the country, is *Praia da Ursa*. At least in summer, the Caparica beaches and at a stretch, Guincho, are accessible by bus or train and bus. *www.beachcam.pt*

The marble mosaic showing Portugal's former colonies, in front of the Padrão dos Descobrimentos

deira | www.mnetnologia-ipmuseus.pt |
bus 732 to Avenida Ilha Madeira

6 MUSEU DA PRESIDÊNCIA
(127 D5) (*D11*)

The Belém Palace shelters the Museum of the Presidency, documenting Portugal's presidents since becoming a republic, from the first one, the modest intellectual Manuel Arriaga, who hated to see money wasted (1910), to Anibal Cavaco Silva, the current one. Come INSIDERTIP▶ at the weekend, when you can take in the palace, the gardens and the Virgin Mary Cycle of Portugal's most famous living artist, Paula Rego. *Museum Tue–Sun 10am–6pm |2.50 euros; palace and gardens Sat 10.30am–5.30pm, Sun 2–4.30pm | 5 euros (free Sun mornings) | Praça Afonso de Albuquerque| www.museu.presidencia.pt | eléctrico 15*

7 PADRÃO DOS DESCOBRIMENTOS
🌿 (126 C6) (*C12*)

Symbolising the departure of the Portuguese explorers for new worlds, this huge white monument was erected beside the river in Belém in 1960 to commemorate Prince Henry the Seafarer (*Infante Dom Henrique*, 1394–1460), on the occasion of the 500-year anniversary of his death. At 50m (164ft) high, the monument pushes out into the Tagus like the prow of a caravel. On top of it stands Henry the Navigator, whose mythical school for seafarers in Sagres (Algarve) formed the nucleus of the Discoveries. Clustering behind him in the line-up of figures are important personalities of the day: captains, kings, astronomers, writers. A lift takes visitors up to the viewing platform, for the best view over the large marble mosaic on the ground in front of the monument. It shows a map of the world with the former Portuguese colonies clearly marked. The audiovisual *Lisboa Experience* forms part of the package. *Tue–Sun 10am–5pm | admission 2.50 euros | www.padraodosdescubrimentos.egeac.pt | eléctrico 15 to Centro Cultural Belém*

8 PALÁCIO NACIONAL DA AJUDA
(127 D2–3) (𝔐 D10)

While King João VI commissioned the palace in 1802, it was 1862 by the time King Luís I moved into the new royal residence with his queen Dona Maria Pia. It was never to be truly finished. The young queen took responsibility for designing the interior, and the palace is exquisitely furnished with unusual antiquities and works of art. In the pink-hued Saxon Hall, even the chairs and tables are manufactured from Meissen porcelain. A few rooms are still used for state receptions today. *Thu–Tue 10am–5.30pm | admission 5 euros (Sun free until 2pm) | www.palaciodaajuda. imc-ip.pt | eléctrico 18 to Calçada Ajuda (Palácio)*

9 TORRE DE BELÉM ★ ☀
(126 A6) (𝔐 B12)

This defensive tower in fine Manueline style is a reminder of the time when the Portuguese explorers started their sea journeys on caravels from here. Built under the aegis of King Manuel I between 1515 and 1521, the tower served more as a welcoming symbol for ships coming back from all corners of the world, laden with goods, rather than for defending the wide mouth of the river. The original position of this historic gem used to be on a small island in the middle of the Tagus. Over the course of the centuries, the river silted up, so that today the Torre is accessible from the shore. A short footbridge leads inside, past a few cannons, and on to the terrace with the statue of the patron saint of success, Madona do Bom Sucesso, who used to greet the ships of the explorers all those centuries ago. From a height of 35m(115ft) the fourth floor affords a good view of the surroundings and the river. In high season it gets fairly claustrophobic up here. *Oct–April Tue–Sun 10am–5.30pm, May–Sept Tue–Sun 10am–6.30pm | admission 5 euros (free Sun until 2pm) | www.torrebelem. pt | eléctrico 15 to Largo da Princesa*

OUTSIDE THE CITY CENTRE

AQUEDUTO DAS ÁGUAS LIVRES
(125 D2–3) (𝔐 H6)

The *Aqueduct of the Free Waters* is one of the most imposing icons of the capital. Even though Lisbon is practically surrounded by the delta of the river Tagus, lack of drinking water was the city's main problem for centuries. While King D. João V. (1705–1750) commissioned the aqueduct, his people paid for it with a water tax. The water was channelled across 18km (11mi) both below and above ground to the *Mãed'Água* (Mother of the Water) reservoir close to today's Amoreiras shopping centre. Miraculously, the monumental structure survived the earthquake of 1755 intact, and the aqueduct remained in use until 1967. Spanning just under 1km (half a mile), the section that bridges the Alcântara Valley forms the most impressive part of the structure. It consists of 35 arches, the tallest of which is 65m (213ft) high and 29m (95ft) wide. After a period of restoration works, the INSIDER TIP footpath across the aqueduct may once again be open to pedestrians. While it can only be crossed in one direction, it offers excellent views. *1 March–30 Nov Mon–Sat 10am–6pm | admission 2.50 euros | Calçada da Quintinha, 6 | bus 702 from Marquês de Pombal to Cç. Mestres*

MUSEU DE ARTE POPULAR
(126 B6) (𝔐 C12)

Reopened in 2012, the Folk Art Museum presents popular art from all over Portugal and also changing exhibitions about popular culture. Check the website for up-to date opening hours and admission charges (between 2 and 9 euros); the shop is an excellent place to buy original presents and souvenirs. *Av. de Brasília | www.map.imc-ip.pt | eléctrico 15E to Belém*

CRISTO REI ☙ (134 C4) (*⌘ O*)

With his gaze fixed firmly towards Lisbon, the statue of Christ on the southern banks of the Tagus receives his visitors with open arms. For some, the Christ King is a place of pilgrimage, but most people come here for the spectacular views over Lisbon and the delta of the Tagus. A lift whisks visitors up 80m (262ft) to the viewing platform supporting the 28m-high (92ft) concrete statue. Inaugurated in 1959, the figure of Christ, a copy of the Redemptor in Rio de Janeiro, was erected in gratitude for Portugal having been spared the World War II. *In winter daily 9.30am–6.15pm, in summer Mon–Fri 9.30am–6.30pm, Sat/Sun until 7pm | admission 4 euros | www.cristorei. pt | ferry from Cais do Sodré to Cacilhas, then bus 101 to Cristo Rei*

MUSEU DE CALOUSTE GULBENKIAN
⭐ (120 A4) (*⌘ K5*)

Many consider the city's largest museum to be the most beautiful. The Gulbenkian shows part of the art collection that Armenian oil magnate Calouste Sarkis Gulbenkian bequeathed to Lisbon, which had provided him with a safe haven during the World War II. Half of the exhibition shows Oriental applied arts and crafts – tapestries, azulejos, carpets, books and manuscripts, porcelain and glassware from Turkey, Persia, Syria and China. Further rooms display paintings and sculptures of European masters, which are kept in a subdued light, with occasional glimpses of outside greenery. You'll find works by Rubens, Rembrandt, Frans Hals, Turner, Gainsborough, Manet, Degas, Renoir and Rodin, as well as period furniture, porcelain and silver tableware, most of them masterpieces in the 18th-century French tradition. Fans of Art Nouveau may want to spend a large part of their visit in the room dedicated to René Lalique.

A stroll through the pretty ⬤ Gulbenkian gardens and a visit to the adjacent *Centro de Arte Monderna* (Museum of Modern Art), which provides an overview of the modern and contemporary art scene in Portugal, are well worth it. *Tue–Sun 10am–5.45pm | admission 4 euros (free admission on Sun), combination ticket with Centro de Arte Monderna 7 euros |*

Lisbon's largest and arguably most beautiful museum, Museu de Calouste Gulbenkian

Avenida de Berna, 45A | www.museu.gul benkian.pt | Metro (blue) São Sebastião

MUSEU DA CIDADE (119 F2) (*∅ O*)

This is the story of the city from antiquity to the current day. Especially interesting is an interactive 3D model showing Lisbon before the 1755 earthquake. The city museum is housed in the *Palácio Pimenta*, which King João V had erected in 1746 as a present for his mistress. The inside of the palace alone, with its furniture and splendid azulejos, as well as the beautiful old palace kitchen, is well worth visiting. Contemporary art exhibitions take place in an adjacent pavilion. New since 2011: the museum's garden has become the *Jardim Bordallo (see also 'Travel with Kids')* with fabulously surreal animal sculptures. *Tue–Sun 10am–1pm, 2–6pm | admission 2.76 euros | Campo Grande, 245 | Metro (yellow, green) Campo Grande*

MUSEU NACIONAL DO AZULEJO ★
(133 D3–4) (*∅ P–Q7*)

Even though it is not on the Metro system, this tile museum really is a must-see. Boasting a comprehensive collection of azulejos from Portugal, the Netherlands and Spain, it offers an interesting cross-section of the historic development of the art of tile painting that is so typical of Portugal – from Moorish beginnings into the 21st century. An azulejo panorama 35m (115ft) long and showing Lisbon before the earthquake occupies pride of place in the collection. The museum is housed in the *Convento da Madre de Deus* built in 1509, though today only its Manueline portal remains in place. The restored nave of the church and the vestry show a wealth of baroque gilded wood carvings (talha dourada). The pretty café-restaurant with its courtyard terrace is worth a visit too. On hot days, this is a lovely, restful spot shaded by palm trees. *Tue 2–6pm, Wed–Sun 10am–noon, 2–6pm (café open at lunchtime) | admission 3 euros | ● Sun 10am–noon | free admission | Rua Madre de Deus, 4 | www.mnazulejo.imc-ip.pt | bus 794 to Igreja Madre Deus*

MUSEU DO ORIENTE (128 C5) (*∅ H11*)

The imposing Museum of the Orient tells the story of the Portuguese presence in Asia. Antiquities, paintings and art objects illustrate the great era of the Portuguese explorers. The second floor is completely given over to the gods of Asia. On display are costumes, puppets, masks, paintings and ritual items. The museum also puts on a varied cultural programme of workshops, music, theatre, dance, cinema and changing exhibitions, plus an Oriental restaurant. *Closed Tue, on other days 10am–6pm, Fri to 10pm | admission 4 euros (● Fri 6–10pm free of charge) | Avenida Brasília | Doca de Alcântara | www.museudooriente.pt | eléctrico 15E, 18E, bus 12, 28, 714, 738, 742 to Alcântara Mar (Museu Oriente)*

PALÁCIO DOS MARQUESES DE FRONTEIRA (124 B1) (*∅ G5*)

The romantic gardens are what most draw the eye in this noble palace in the Benfica part of town. The first Marquis of Fronteira commissioned the palace in the 17th century, initially as a hunting pavilion. Particularly impressive are the azulejos. Deities, planets, signs of the zodiac, birds, cats and monkeys adorn benches and façades on the veranda. The magnificently tiled Kings Gallery dominates the lower part of the gardens. The azulejos shine deep dark blue in the sun and find their reflection in the pond in front. *Only accessible on a guided tour, June–Sept Mon–Sat 10.30, 11, 11.30am, noon, Oct–May Mon–Sat 11am and noon | admission palace and gardens 7.50, gardens 3 euros | Largo São Domingos de Benfica, 1 | www.fronteira-alorna. pt | Metro (blue) Jardim Zoológico, then bus 70 to Palácio Fronteira*

ing and energy-efficient mosaic covering reminiscent of fish scales. The futuristic *Pavilhão Atlântico* can hold 20,000 people for concerts and sports events. Next door you'll find the trade fair grounds of

Fishwatching: the Oceanário is the top visitor attraction in the Park of Nations

PARQUE DAS NAÇÕES (PARK OF NATIONS) ★ ●
(117 E–F 1–4) (*Ø S1–4*)

The World Exposition of 1998 formed part of a gigantic urbanisation project, and the former Expo area has become a symbol for the new Lisbon. A new neighbourhood emerged on the banks of the Tagus, practically from wasteland; today, some 20,000 people live and work here. This is also where you'll find Lisbon's gems of contemporary architecture, like pearls on a string. The 17km (10mi) *Ponte Vasco da Gama* spans the wide Tagus delta. An architectural highlight is the high-tech train station of *Oriente*: a filigree palm grove made from steel and glass, designed by Spanish star architect Santiago Calatrava.

The number one attraction in Park of Nations is the gigantic ● *Oceanário*, Europe's second-largest marine aquarium (*see 'Travel with Children'*). In 2011, a new south wing was added, its shimmer-

FIL Feira Internacional de Lisboa. Alongside numerous bars and pubs, the Casino Lisboa , which also stages shows and has a luxury restaurant, draws visitors in the evening. To explore the area more actively, hire bikes or rollerblades *(www. tejobike.pt)*, or join a Segway tour *(www. redtourgps.com)*. *www.portaldasnacoes. pt | Metro (red) Oriente*

PARQUE FLORESTAL DE MONSANTO
(124 A–C 1–6) (*Ø C–G 5–10*)

This huge park in the northwest of Lisbon boasts endless biking, hiking and riding trails, picnic spots, playgrounds, fitness trails and a few restaurants. There are also free-climbing and skating facilities. Monsanto now forms part of a newly laid out, 14km (8.5mi) long 'Biodiversity Route', leading past places of interest for history, natural history and ecology. The starting point is in Belém *(www. lisboaverde.cm-lisboa.pt)*. *Bus 729 from Belém to Montes Claros*

The Atlantic beaches of Estoril and Cascais already face the open sea

PONTE 25 DE ABRIL

(128 B6) (*Ø G11–12*)

The elegant Ponte 25 (*Vinte e cinco*) de Abril is strongly reminiscent of the Golden Gate Bridge in San Francisco. Dictator Salazar bestowed his own name on the bridge when it was inaugurated in 1966. After the regime was toppled, the bridge was given its current name to commemorate the Carnation Revolution of 25 April 1974. The five-lane highway across the river is at a height of 70m (230ft); the rail track underneath the road was added in 1999.

DAY TRIPS

ESTORIL/CASCAIS (134 A3–4) (*Ø O*)

On the coast 25km (15mi) west of Lisbon, Estoril and Cascais used to be the seaside resorts of choice for kings and nobility. The train ride from Lisbon's Cais do Sodré station takes only half an hour or so, but it's worth allocating a whole day to visit the resorts, if you don't want to rush it. Bring swimming togs!

Estoril is famous, and not only for having the biggest casino in Europe. During World War Two, the town was swarming with spies, as well as receiving many prominent personalities and royalty. From Estoril, you can take a wonderful walk along the beach promenade to Cascais.

Cascais has managed to hold on to the charm of its historic centre. The vibrant old part of Cascais – which, by the way, is home to a sizeable British and Irish population – has many bars, restaurants and boutiques. The City Hall (*Câmara Municipal*) boasts a fine *azulejo* façade. On the steep southern shore, the mighty citadel juts out into the sea. Nearby *Parque Marechal Carmona* city park, has small ponds and hothouses, as well as playgrounds. The park leads on to the maritime museum, Museu do Mar, which tells the story of the region's seafaring traditions *(Tue–Sun 10am–5pm | admission 2.20 euros)*. Next door, the INSIDER TIP Paula Rego Museum, celebrates the fascinating work of the London-based Portuguese artist. A 1km (half a mile) walk along the coast road (or ride on one of the free bikes available from the station or citadel) leads to the natural spectacle of *Boca do Inferno*, the 20m (65ft) deep 'Mouth of Hell'. Five kilometres (3mi) north, discover one of Portugal's most beautiful beaches – the *Praia do Guincho*, known to windsurfers the world over. One of their favourite meeting spots is the INSIDERTIP Bar do Guincho *(daily to late at night)* right on the beach. Information: *www.estorilcoast.cos*

SINTRA (134 B3) (*O*)

This picturesque little town – very popular with British expats – occupies a scenic position at the foot of the Sintra hills, 20km (12mi) west of Lisbon. The town has many places to visit, including royal palaces and stately homes, parks and gardens. The train ride from Lisbon's Rossio station takes approximately 45 minutes. Since Sintra joined the Unesco World Heritage list in 1995, the town, which has about 24,000 inhabitants, has received even more visitors, and admission prices are steep. It's worth enquiring about cheaper multi-entry tickets. Sintra's emblem, the *Palácio Nacional de Sintra (Thu–Tue 10am–5pm | admission 5 euros)* stands out with its huge conical chimneys. For generations, this 16th-century palace was used as a summer residence by Portugal's royal family.

A reminder of that era is the unique tiled walls showing hunting and picnic scenes. High above Sintra, the *Palácio Nacional da Pena (daily, April–Sept 10am–7pm, admission 11 euros, Oct–March 10am–6pm, admission 8 euros)* is a fairy-tale castle in the vein of Bavaria's Neuschwanstein, surrounded by a picturesque park. *Cruz Alta* (High Cross), the highest point of the Sintra hills (529m/1735ft), affords a unique panoramic vista. The castle itself, a romantic mix of Gothic, Baroque, Manueline, Renaissance and Moorish architecture, is accessible by taxi, by bus No. 434 or on foot. The walk through the INSIDERTIP fairy-tale woods takes about one hour. The Turismo has hiking maps.

From Sintra, it is just under 15km (9mi) on the EN247 to *Cabo da Roca*, the rocky cape that forms the westernmost point of the European continent. A lighthouse rises high above the Atlantic, and the sunsets here are spectacular. The INSIDERTIP *Moninho Don Quixote windmill*, converted into a terrace bar in *Azoia*, shortly before you reach Cabo da Roca, makes a great refuelling stop. Information: *Turismo Sintra | tel. 219231157 | www.cm-sintra.pt*

KEEP FIT!

There are two fine and exhaust-fume free routes for runners: the first runs along the Expo compound **(117 F1–4)** (*S1–4*). Getting up early is worth it for an early-morning jog in the *Parque das Nações*, on the knee-friendly boardwalk along the 'Sea of Straw', in the shadow of impressive contemporary architecture. The second leads from the transport hub of *Cais do Sodré* **(130 C6)** (*L10*) 6km (4mi) to Belém along the Tagus, taking in sights such as the *Torre de Belém*, the Discoveries Monument and the Hieronymite Monastery. Those preferring to run under professional supervision and take in some sightseeing along the way, can choose from three one-hour runs at *Jogging Tours*. *Rua dos Douradores 16* **(131 D5)** (*N9*) | *tel. 210965030 | www.jogging-tours.com | Metro (blue) Terreiro do Paço*

FOOD & DRINK

Traditional Portuguese cuisine is simple, rustic and hearty. Portions are usually generous. A hefty plate of fish or meat is complemented with rice and potatoes (often at the same time), plus a few lettuce leaves as standard garnish.

Sometimes you might find the unusual in the most simple of eateries *(tascas)*, where the *dona* of the house still cooks personally, lovingly following handed-down family recipes.

The country's economic difficulties haven't been all bad for Lisbon's gastronomy. Young Portuguese chefs who earned their spurs abroad – think of Nuno Mendes' Viajante in London – bring back innovative ideas and breathe fresh air into the capital's gastronomic scene. Lunch *(almoço)* is usually served between 1 and 3pm, while dinner *(jantar)* is served from about 8pm (though most diners arrive one or two hours later – the same holds true for dinner parties, by the way). At 8pm, you'll probably get a table anywhere, even without booking; otherwise it's advisable to reserve at the more fancy restaurants, especially at the weekend. The appetisers appearing on the cover charge *(couvert)* such as olives, cheese, tuna pâté, bread and butter are charged, so ask for them to be removed if you don't want them.

The national dish is codfish, *bacalhau*, which the Portuguese like to call their faithful friend *(o fiel amigo)*. There are said to be at least 365 different ways to prepare it. Tasty, cheap and a popular favourite, grilled sardines *(sardinhas assadas)* are rubbed with coarse sea salt and grilled

Photo: Bacalhau with potatoes and olives

The Atlantic is the larder of Portugal –
take the chance while in town to taste
the superb fresh fish and seafood dishes

over charcoal *(na brasa)*. Fans of shellfish *(mariscos)* will enjoy the *marisqueiras* (seafood restaurants). While the variety is impressive, do watch the (kilo) price. Lobster *(lavagante)* and crayfish *(lagostas)* aren't cheap in Lisbon either.

Vegetarians are looked after well in ethnic restaurants, and the more expensive Portuguese restaurants, but they will have a harder time in the traditional eateries. Waiters often panic when you tell them you don't eat meat or fish – and might suggest tuna – and if you ask for the vegeta-

ble sides, chefs sometimes refuse to serve them, with the excuse that they wouldn't know what to charge. Omelettes, fries and salads are a trusty if unexciting standby. Organic produce and free-range eggs are hard to find outside supermarkets.

The Portuguese like their meat *(carne)* to be well done. Lamb *(borrego)* is a favourite choice. Another popular dish is crispy suckling pig *(leitão assado)*, which is offered in many basic eateries (e. g. at INSIDERTIP *A Merendinha, Rua Condes de Monsanto 4-A, at Praça da Figueira)*. A speciality worth look-

CAFÉS

ing out for is *porco preto* from the Alentejo region south of Lisbon, an acorn-fed 'black pig'. If you like poultry, order the tasty grilled chicken *(frango assado)*, or for a spicier version, *piripiri*. The desserts *(sobremesas)* are good but often very sweet. Popular options include sweet rice *(arroz doce)*, caramel pudding *(pudim flan)*, like a crème caramel, and milk custard *(leite creme)*. Make sure you try the specialities of Portugal's former colonies, including Goa and Cape Verde. Lisbon has many good Brazilian, Indian, African and Chinese restaurants.

Wine lovers will have plenty of choice. Whether red *(vinho tinto)* or white wine *(vinho branco)*, there is always a good range available, and prices are low. A mid-range bottle *(garrafa)* ordered in a regular restaurant will cost about 8–12 euros. The house wine *(vinho da casa)* is even cheaper and usually pretty decent. The slighty bubbly *vinho verde* should only be enjoyed chilled *(bem fresco)*.

Pessoa, who was a regular here. In front of the café a bronze statue of the great man sitting at a table has pride of place. Go inside if you want a less-touristy atmosphere. Late at night, night owls meet here to sip their espresso. One more thing: Bénard next door sells Lisbon's

Pastéis de Belém: fresh out of the oven, the custard tarts are hard to resist

best croissants. *Rua Garrett, 120 | Metro (blue, green) Baixa-Chiado*

CAFÉ LINHA D'ÁGUA (120 A5) *(𝄞 K6)*

Above the Eduardo VII city park, not far from the Corte Inglés department store, this airy cafeteria with a pretty terrace is situated in the Amália Rodrigues garden, overlooking a small lake. A studenty clientele (hardly any tourists) and friendly self-service. *Rua Marquês da Fronteira | Metro (blue) São Sebastião*

CAFÉ MARTINHO DA ARCADA (131 D5) *(𝄞 N10)*

Lisbon's oldest café was inaugurated in 1782 by the Marquês de Pombal. Again, Fernando Pessoa was a regular here, and would sometimes pay for his aguardente with poems. Today, Portuguese cuisine is served alongside coffee and cakes. It is a popular haunt of

CAFÉS

CAFÉ A BRASILEIRA ● (130 C5) *(𝄞 M9)*

Lisbon's most famous café, the 'Brazilian' owes its fame to the poet Fernando

politicians from the surrounding ministries. *Praça do Comércio, 3 | Metro (blue, green) Baixa-Chiado*

CONFEITARIA NACIONAL
(131 D4) (𝓜 M9)

The oldest pastry shop in town (1829) is a great meeting point for an afternoon coffee and a chat. In the winter, try a yeasty bolo rei. *Praça da Figueira, 18 | Metro (green) Rossio*

PÃO DE CANELA (130 B4) (𝓜 K–L9)

This cosy café-restaurant with terrace on lovely Praça das Flores has a faithful following. Artists, journalists, deputies from the nearby parliament and the bairro neighbours all enjoy the relaxed atmosphere under shady trees. Basic cooking, breakfasts too. *Praça das Flores 25/29 | bus 773 to Praça das Flores*

SANTINI (131 D4–5) (𝓜 M9)

With its super-central location and long opening hours, the new branch of the legendary Cascais ice-cream parlour draws long queues. You can also pair a coffee with good chocolate cake or the tasty Tarte Santini. *Daily 10am–midnight | Rua do Carmo 9 | www.santini.pt | Metro (blue) Restauradores or (green) Rossio*

ÚNICA FÁBRICA PASTÉIS DE BELÉM
(126 C5) (𝓜 D11)

Lisbon's most famous pastry has been manufactured here since 1837, to a secret recipe: *pastéis de Belém*, custard pies fresh from the oven. *Rua de Belém, 84 | near Hieronymite Monastery | www.pasteisdebelem.pt | Eléctrico 15 to Bélem*

RESTAURANTS: EXPENSIVE

BICA DO SAPATO ★ 🌿
(132 C6) (𝓜 P9)

This project was the brainchild of Lisbon's avant-garde guru Manuel Reis and Hollywood star John Malkovich. A trendy restaurant in Seventies retro chic, it occupies a former port warehouse. You can look out over the Tagus through the panoramic windows, and there's outdoor seating in summer. Snacks are served in the cafeteria, and sushi on the first floor. Seeing and being seen while enjoying designer cuisine is the name of the game. Look out for set lunch deals. *Closed Sun, as well as Mon lunchtime | Av. Infante D. Henrique | Cais da Pedra | tel. 2 18 81 03 20 | www.bicadosapato.com | Metro (blue) to Santa Apolónia*

★ **Bica do Sapato**
Wealthy hipsters get together in this former warehouse → p. 59

★ **A Travessa**
In the summer, you can eat in the monastery's cloisters → p. 61

★ **Cervejaria da Trindade**
Tuck into tapas with a beer in this former monastery church in Bairro Alto → p. 63

★ **Santo António**
Rub shoulders with artists and media folk in Alfama → p. 64

★ **Alma**
Come here for trendy 'soul food' – gourmet food at good prices → p. 61

★ **Tavares**
Fine dining in Lisbon's oldest luxury restaurant → p. 60

MARCO POLO HIGHLIGHTS

BOCCA (130 A2) (📖 K7)

This is the new hotspot for the wealthy. It offers creative Portuguese and international gourmet cuisine, yet has an easy-going feel and modern ambience. At lunchtime its three-course 27-euro lunch ('Executive Menu') is popular with the city's suits. Has a good wine list, too. *Closed Sun/Mon | Rua Rodrigo da Fonseca, 87D | tel. 21380 83 83 | www.bocca.pt | Metro (blue, yellow) Marquês de Pombal*

ESTORIL MANDARIM ⚜ (134 A3–4) (📖 O)

This restaurant, owned by gambling tycoon Stanley Ho from Macao, offers authentic Chinese cuisine in a subtly elegant ambience. It is located in the casino building and has fine views across the park. The casino also hosts fado, jazz and pop music greats, plus dance revue shows. On summer Thursdays, from 11.30pm, concerts are held in the garden. *Closed Mon/Tue | Praça José Teodoro dos Santos | Casino Estoril | tel. 2 14 66 72 70 | www.casino-estoril.pt | train from Cais do Sodré to Estoril*

FAZ FIGURA ⚜ (132 C6) (📖 O9)

This is one of Lisbon's classic restaurants, with beautiful view across the Tagus. Its light-filled conservatory and terrace

GOURMET RESTAURANTS

Eleven ⚜ (120 A6) (📖 K6)

German-born Michelin-star chef Joachim Körper serves Mediterranean cuisine in luxurious surroundings with a modern ambience. Gorgeous views across the city and the Tagus too. À la carte 65 euros. *Closed Sun | Rua Marquês de Fronteira, Jardim Amália Rodrigues | tel. 2 13 86 22 11 | www.restauranteleven. com | Metro (blue) São Sebastião*

Gambrinus (131 D4) (📖 M8–9)

This veteran of the Lisbon gastro scene oozes refined 1960s charm. Seafood, fish and game are specialities. À la carte 50 euros. *Daily | Rua das Portas de Santo Antão 23 | tel. 2 13 42 14 66 | www.gam brinuslisboa.com | Metro (green) Rossio*

Tavares ⭐ (130 C5) (📖 M9)

This is the most famous and oldest (1784!) luxury restaurant in town. Enjoy international cuisine under gilded stucco ceilings. Their current top chef is the young and innovative José Avillez. À la carte 65 euros. *Closed Sat and Mon lunch, as well as Sun | Rua da Misericórdia 37 | tel. 2 13 42 11 12 | www.tavares rico.pt | Metro (blue, green) Baixa-Chiado*

Valle Flôr (128 A 4) (📖 F10)

The restaurant of the *Pestana Palace* hotel is a favourite with Lisbon's VIPs. French head chef Aimé Barroyer lends a creative touch to traditional dishes. À la carte 70 euros. *Daily | Rua Jau, 54 | tel. 2 13 61 56 00 | www.pestana.com | eléctrico 18 to Alto Santo Amaro*

Varanda do Ritz (130 A1) (📖 K7)

This has been a meeting point for Lisbon's high society since the 1960s. In summer, an excellent lunch buffet is served on the terrace. Mediterranean cuisine. À la carte 50 euros. *Daily | Rua Rodrigo da Fonseca 88 | tel. 2 13 81 14 00 | www.fourseasons.com | Metro (blue, yellow) Marquês de Pombal*

make it a favourite meeting place for wealthy Lisbon families. It offers fine Portuguese and international cuisine, including vegetarian dishes. Very friendly service. *Daily | tel. 21886 89 81 | Alfama | Rua do Paraíso, 15B | www.fazfigura.com | bus 12 to Rua do Paraíso*

RESTAURANTE 100 MANEIRAS
(130 C4) (*Ø L9*)

At this trendsetting Bairro Alto restaurant, Bosnian star chef Ljubomir Stanisic serves up Portuguese-Mediterranean cuisine that would well merit a Michelin star – thankfully without the prices. There is no à la carte, but the tasting menus *(40 euros) are superb.* A fun appetiser: bacalhau strips on miniature washing lines. If money is no object, choose the option offering matching Portuguese wines with each course; the white wines are particularly good. There's a cheaper bistro-style branch nearby, too. *Rua do Teixeira 35 | tel. 210 99 04 75 or 910 30 75 75 | www.restaurante100maneiras.com | Metro (green) Rossio or (blue) Restauradores, then Elevador da Glória or on foot*

A TRAVESSA ★
(129 E–F 3–4) (*Ø K10*)

This long-established restaurant is run by the Portuguese-Belgian duo Vivien and António in the former Bernardas monastery in the Madragoa part of town. The tasty hors-d'œuvres, which automatically arrive at your table, are Travessa's calling card. The Saturday night speciality is mussels *(mexilhões)*. In summer, operations are moved into the open-air cloisters. Service is attentive and friendly, and the guests a *Who's Who* of Portugal. *Closed Sat lunchtime and Sun | Travessa do Convento das Bernardas, 12 | tel. 213 90 20 34 or 213 94 08 00 | www.atravessa.com | Eléctrico 25 to Santos-o-Velho*

ALMA ★ (130 A5) (*Ø K10*)

The soul *(alma)* of this new restaurant is the well-known TV chef Henrique Sá Pessoa. With this stylish eatery, offering international gourmet cuisine with a Portuguese touch, he has clearly hit the

Eleven, a top choice for fine dining

zeitgeist. The prices are reasonable, with a tasting menu, for instance, at 29 euros. *Evenings only, closed Sun/Mon | Calçada do Marquês de Abrantes, 92–94 | tel. 213 96 35 27 | www.alma.co.pt | Eléctrico 25 to Largo Vitorino Damásio*

ATIRA-TE AO RIO ॐ (134 C4) (*Ø O*)

When the sun goes down over Lisbon, this is the place to be. The name of the restaurant on the other side of the Tagus translates as 'Throw yourself into the River'. Relax in one of the lounge chairs on the riverside terrace, cocktail in hand,

LOCAL SPECIALITIES

▶ **açorda de marisco** – bread stew with seafood

▶ **amêijoas à bulhão pato** – mussels in a garlic-lemon sauce

▶ **arroz de pato** – rice with duck

▶ **bacalhau à brás** – codfish potato gratin

▶ **bife à Marrare** – fillet of beef in a garlic and cream sauce

▶ **bitoque** – steak with fried egg and chips/fries

▶ **bolo-Rei** – 'King's Cake', Christmas and Easter cake made with dried fruit

▶ **cabrito** – kid goat, prepared with fresh herbs

▶ **caldeirada à fragateira** – fish stew with tomatoes and potato

▶ **caldo verde** – soup made from green cabbage and potato

▶ **cerveja** – beer

▶ **chanfana** – goat in wine sauce

▶ **cozido à portuguesa** – hearty stew of various cuts of meat and vegetables (photo right)

▶ **favas à moda de Lisboa** – fava beans with bacon and sausage

▶ **feijoada à portuguesa** – bean stew with sausage

▶ **frango na púcara** – chicken, prepared in a clay pot

▶ **iscas com elas** – liver with spleen

▶ **lulas recheadas** – stuffed squid

▶ **pão-de-ló** – biscuit cake

▶ **pastéis de bacalhau** – fried codfish pasties

▶ **pastéis de Belém** – custard tarts (photo left)

▶ **peixinhos da horta** – fried green beans in tempura

▶ **porco à alentejana** – pork goulash with mussels

▶ **queijadas de Sintra** – sweet curd pastries from Sintra

▶ **rissóis de camarão** – fried prawn rissoles

▶ **salada de polvo** – octopus salad

admiring the view over the city. It is lovely in the afternoon as well. *Closed Mon | Cais Gingal 69 | tel. 2 12 75 13 80 | www. atirateaorio.pt | ferry from Cais do Sodré to Cacilhas, then about 10 min. on foot, turning right along the quay*

O CANTINHO DA PAZ (130 A–B5) (*Ø K9*)
This cosy family-run restaurant specialises in dishes from the former Indo-Portuguese colony of Goa. The host Sebastião enjoys entertaining his guests – artists, journalists and politicians from

the nearby parliament – with care and the occasional joke. The restaurant's chic offshoot *Casa da Goa (daily | Calçada do Livramento, 17 | tel. 21 3 93 01 71 (128 C4) (𝘔 H10))* has been crowned the best ethnic restaurant in town. *Closed Sun | Rua da Paz, 4 | tel. 21 3 90 19 63 | eléctrico 28 to Rua Poiais de São Bento*

INSIDER TIP ▶ CASA DA MORNA
(128 B4) (𝘔 G10)

The Cape Verdean equivalent of the fado is called morna. On the African archipelago, singer Tito Paris is a star, and at his Lisbon restaurant, specialities from the former Portuguese colony are accompanied by soft piano sounds (on Thursdays, Senhor Tito himself plays). There's often dancing too. Why not try the Cape Verdean national dish of *cachupa*, a bean-and-corn stew with meat? The kitchen stays open late – until 1.30am! *Closed Sun | Rua Rodrigues de Faria, 21 | tel. 21 3 64 63 99 | www.casadamorna. com.pt | eléctrico 15, 18 to Calvário*

CERVEJARIA DA TRINDADE ★
(130 C4) (𝘔 M9)

This is the classic place to enjoy a beer in Lisbon. The large rooms form part of a former monastery church. In summer, you can sit in the small shady garden. Whether meat or fish, a whole meal or only a couple of *tapas* (appetisers), there is something to eat most times of the day or night. *Daily 10am–1.30am, Closed on public holidays | Rua Nova da Trindade, 20c | tel. 21 3 42 35 06 | www.cervejariatrindade.pt | Metro (blue, green) Baixa-Chiado*

A MARGEM **(126 B6) (𝘔 C12)**

This minimalist white, glass-encased *esplanada* nestles so discreetly into the riverside panorama that many passers-by don't even notice it. This may change now that the Folk Art Museum next door has opened its doors again. Sit inside or outside and enjoy good wines, classy teas, and snacks and salads on designer plates. Not the fastest service, and very popular at weekends. *Daily | Doca de Bom Sucesso (halfway between the Discoveries Monument and Torre de Belém) | tel. 9 18 22 55 48 | www.amargem.com | eléctrico 15 E, suburban train: Belém*

MERCADO DO PEIXE **(126 C1) (𝘔 D9)**

There's excellent fish and seafood aplenty at this restaurant on Monsanto

A Lisbon institution: the Cervejaria da Trindade

RESTAURANTS: BUDGET

Park. It has a huge charcoal grill, and is large, noisy and very popular. Just as well the waiters are fleet of foot. Watch the kilo price, as it can work out expensive. *Closed Sun eve | Estr. Pedro Teixeira | tel. 213 61 60 70 | www.mercadodopeixe.web. pt | bus 60 from Praça Comércio to Cara-mão da Ajuda*

RESTÔ DO CHAPITÔ ⤵
(131 E4) *(∅ N9)*

A trendy restaurant with fabulous views, this place offers two styles of dining: the first floor serves international cuisine, including vegetarian; the ground-floor serves much cheaper tapas and drinks. In summer, the terrace bar opens daily noon–1.30am. *Rua Costa do Castelo, 7 | tel. 218 86 73 34 | www.chapito.org | Metro (green) Rossio or Eléctrico 28 to Miradouro de Santa Luzia*

LOW BUDGET

▶ The best feature of the Catholic *A.C.I.S.J.F.* canteen, popularly known as 'the nuns' *(as Freiras)* **(130 C5)** *(∅ M10)*, is the terrace. A lunch (self-service) costs just 6.20 euros, snacks 1–2 euros. *Mon–Fri noon–3pm | Travessa do Ferragial 1 | tel. 2 13 24 09 10 | eléctrico 28 to R. Vitor Cordon/R. Serpa Pinto*

▶ For paper-thin pork fillets off the grill *(lombinhos na chapa)*, tiny *Tasca Adega dos Lombinhos* **(131 D5)** *(∅ M–N9)* serves them just right, and a meal will only cost around 6 euros. *Mon–Sat 7am–9pm | Rua dos Douradores, 52 | tel. 2 18 87 80 28 | Metro (blue, green) Baixa-Chiado*

SANTO ANTÓNIO ⭐ (131 E5) *(∅ N9)*
The restaurant next to the São Miguel church has a faithful following: film and media folk, as well as artists appreciate the Alfama ambience. In summer, a small romantic vine-covered terrace is an additional draw. International cuisine. *Daily | Beco de São Miguel, 7 | tel. 218 88 13 28 | www.siteantonio.com | bus 28 to Casa Conto, Metro (blue) Santa Apolónia, then on foot*

RESTAURANTS: BUDGET

ANTIGO 1º DE MAIO (130 C4) *(∅ L9)*
This down-to-earth *tasca* has been a Lisbon staple for decades, acclaimed for its solid fare. However, popularity has taken its toll on quality a bit. *Closed Sat lunch and Sun | Rua da Atalaia, 8 | tel. 213 42 68 40 | Metro (blue, green) Baixa-Chiado*

CASA DO ALENTEJO (130 C3–4) *(∅ M8)*
While the food might be nothing to write home about, the ambience will amaze you. The house representing the Alentejo region south of Lisbon has immense charm. Rustic dishes and **INSIDER TIP** Sunday dancing *(mid-Sept–May Sun 3–7pm, admission 5 euros)*. *Daily | Rua Portas de Santo Antão, 58 | tel. 213 40 51 40 | www.casadoalentejo. pt | Metro (blue) Restauradores*

JARDIM DOS SENTIDOS (130 B3) *(∅ L8)*
This is a good vegetarian restaurant with a friendly vibe and a leafy garden. Come for the good-value buffet lunch. There's also a small organic shop. *Closed Sat lunch and Sun | Rua Mãe d'Água, 3 | tel. 213 42 36 70 (-71) | www. jardimdosentidos.com | Metro (blue) Avenida*

The owner-chef of Antigo 1º de Maio produces tasty home-cooking

INSIDER TIP O MIUDINHO
(118 A1) (*O*)

Get off the beaten track at the Miudinho in Carnide, a charming old-fashioned neighbourhood in the north of Lisbon. Don't let first impressions – a modern development – put you off. The simple restaurant serves traditional Portuguese fare, specialising in meat and fish from the charcoal grill. Large helpings, low prices! *Closed Sun | Rua Neves Costa, 21 | tel. 21714 0120 | Metro (blue) Carnide*

INSIDER TIP SOL E PESCA
(130 C5–6) (*M10*)

This former angling equipment and tinned fish shop in the port quarter – now a hip nightlife mile – has been converted into an informal bar-restaurant .

Choose your tin of fish, pay an additional 2.50 euros for bread and salad, and you're good to go. *Tue–Sat noon–midnight, Fri/Sat sometimes up to 4am | Rua Nova do Carvalho 44 | Metro (green) Cais do Sodré*

TABERNA IDEAL
(130 A5) (*K10*)

The seasonally changing miniature dishes are the hallmark of this new and instantly popular tavern with a vintage look. It's best to book ahead. *Closed Mon, Tue–Fri from 7pm, Sat/Sun from 1.30pm | Rua da Esperança, 112 | Santos | tel. 213 96 27 44 | eléctrico 25 to Largo Vitorino Damásio*

SHOPPING

CITY **WHERE TO START?**
Most shops can be found in downtown **Baixa** (particularly good for shoe stores), in chic **Chiado** and along the two **Avenidas da Liberdade** and **da Roma**. The **Bairro Alto** (Upper Town) has many shops selling quirky fashion, music and eccentric living accessories – while often only opening from 3pm, they then stay open until late at night.

Charmingly nostalgic little shops seemingly untouched by modern times: in Lisbon you'll still find them.

Lisbon's oldest and most traditional stores can often be recognised by the fact that their name and address is inlaid in the pavement outside in black cobblestones. These shops have nearly always been in the same family for generations, and the owners are masters of their profession. Hurry is unknown here. Even if you are only buying a button, choosing the right one can take a while. Once things are finally agreed, the item is wrapped up, *embrulhar* in Portuguese, with loving care. True treasure troves for those with a bit of time on their hands are the tiny haberdashery shops along *Rua da Conceição* in the Baixa.

Things move much faster in the major shopping centres. These modern temples to consumerism on the periphery of the city are much like those in other capital cities: fast food and *fast forward*

In Lisbon, shopping is a real experience, whether in the one-off boutiques of Chiado or in the modern shopping centres

is the order of the day here. While traditional shopping hours are 9am to 7pm with a one-hour break for lunch during the week, and morning-only on Saturday, the shopping centres are open until at least 10pm every day.

Typical products of Portugal are *azulejos* (tiles) and ceramic ware, statues of the gallo (rooster) of Barcelos, embroidery, copper pans, cork and basket ware. Culinary specialities such as Azeitão sheep cheese (eaten by cutting off the top and spooning out the cheese), honey, ol-

ives and wine make good souvenirs for friends and family. Another good buy is the **INSIDER TIP** high-quality olive oil *(azeite)*, sold on every corner. Leather goods and clothing are cheaper than in northern Europe, as is high-grade gold and silver jewellery. Shopaholics may like to invest in the Shopping Card from the tourist offices, which will entitle them to discounts of between 5 and 20 per cent in some 200 shops in the main shopping areas. The card costs 3.70 (valid for 24 hours) or 5.80

Classy, chic and expensive –
the Colombo shopping centre

euros (72 hours). Information: *www. askmelisboa.com*

ANTIQUES

Most antiques shops cluster around the *Rua Dom Pedro V.* and the *Rua de S. Bento.*

ANDRADE (130 C5) (*M10*)
This is a good source of paintings, furniture, European art objects of the 17th and 18th centuries, off the main antiques shops drag. *Rua do Alecrim 48/50 | Metro (blue, green) Baixa-Chiado*

BOOKSHOPS & ANTIQUARIANS

Bookshops cluster between the *Rua do Carmo* and the *Rua Nova do Almada*; this is also where you'll find the big FNAC retail chain.

INSIDER TIP FÁBULA URBIS ●
(131 E5) (*N9*)
This well-stocked bookshop a stone's throw from the cathedral sells titles on Lisbon and Portugal in all the major languages – novels, poetry, history, azulejo guides, cookbooks – and its knowledgeable staff can dispense advice. The top floor sometimes puts on exhibitions or free recitals. *Daily 10am–2pm, 3–8pm | Rua de Augusto Rosa 27 | www.fabula-urbis.pt | bus 12, eléctrico 28*

LER DEVAGAR (128 B4) (*G10*)
The 'Read Slowly' bookshop is always right on trend. The most recent branch is in the current INSIDER TIP cultural hotspot LX Factory (*www.lxfactory.com*). This friendly café operates a permissive smoking policy, and often stages concerts of experimental music on the upper floor. *Mon–Thu noon–midnight, Fri/Sat noon–2am, Sun 3–10pm | Rua Rodrigues Faria, 103 | Alcântara | www.lerdevagar.com | eléctrico 15/18 to Calvário*

LIVRARIA BARATEIRA (130 C4) (*M9*)
Solid antiquarian. *Rua Nova da Trindade 26 | Metro (blue, green) Baixa-Chiado*

SHOPPING CENTRES

AMOREIRAS SHOPPING CENTER ●
(125 E4–5) (*J7*)
This postmodern high-rise complex with 275 shops, 50 restaurants, a supermarket and 10 cinema screens is a major draw for lisboetas. *Daily to 11pm | Av. Eng. Duarte Pacheco | best: bus 711, or Metro (yellow) Marquês de Pombal, Rato, then a 15-min walk*

CENTRO COMERCIAL COLOMBO ●
(118 A2–3) (*O*)
One of the biggest shopping centres in Europe, Colombo offers shops, restau-

rants, cinemas and bowling. It also has a new garden. *Daily 9am–midnight Uhr | Benfica | Metro (blue) Colégio Militar/Luz*

CENTRO COMERCIAL VASCO DA GAMA ★ (117 E3) *(∅ R–S2)*

The modern shopping mall, in avant-garde design with lots of natural light, is situated right on the Parque das Nações, the former Expo area. It has an excellent selection of clothes stores, a supermarket, terrace bars with river view, and cinemas. *Metro (red) Oriente*

GLASSWARE & CERAMICS

DEPÓSITO DA MARINHA GRANDE (130 A4) *(∅ K9)*

Everything here is made from glass, from the simple shot glass to objets d'art. *Rua de São Bento 242/243 und 418–420 | www.dmg.com.pt | bus 706 to Rua São Bento*

SANT'ANNA ★ (127 E4) *(∅ E11)*

This is one of the oldest ceramics and azulejo manufacturers in the city. Shop: (130 C5) *(∅ M9–10) | Rua do Alecrim, 95 | Metro: Baixa-Chiado.* At the factory, visitors are allowed to watch production and, by previous appointment on certain dates, wield the paintbrush themselves. Made-to-order service available. *Mon–Fri 10–12.30pm and 2–6pm | Calçada da Boa-Hora 96 | tel. 2 13 63 82 92 | www.fabrica-santanna.com | bus 732 to Boa-Hora*

VISTA ALEGRE ★ (130 C5) *(∅ M9)*

Pretty Portuguese porcelain makes a fine souvenir, and this is the best place to buy it. No self-respecting Portuguese household is without a service made by this traditional porcelain manufacturer, which used to supply the Portuguese court. The chain (as well as the glass manufacture Atlantis) is also represent-ed at the airport and in most shopping centres. *Largo do Chiado 20–23 | www.vistaalegre.pt | www.vistaalegreatlantis.com | Metro (blue, green) Baixa-Chiado*

CRAFTS & SOUVENIRS

CORK & CO (130 C5) *(∅ L–M9)*

Original cork products – umbrellas, bags, jewellery and much more – are on offer at this cool shop, which, in typically Bairro Alto, fashion doesn't open until 2pm, yet stays open very late, at least in summer. *Rua das Salgadeiras 10 | www.corkandcompany.pt | Metro (blue, green) Baixa-Chiado*

★ **Centro Comercial Vasco da Gama**
Architecturally impressive shopping centre → p. 69

★ **Sant'Anna**
Gorgeous azulejos, including tailor-made on request → p. 69

★ **Vista Alegre**
Finest china from the former purveyor to the court → p. 69

★ **A Vida Portuguesa**
This is the ultimate shop for all fans of nostalgia and retro design → p. 70

★ **Feira da Ladra**
A flea market offering hours of browsing with lots of local colour → p. 70

★ **Solar do Vinho do Porto**
Calm surroundings for those who like to try a few ports before choosing → p. 73

MARCO POLO HIGHLIGHTS

A LOJA (131 D4) (𝄞 N9)
Originally from Paris, photographer MG de Saint-Venant sells a fine selection of vintage clothing, unusual Portuguese crafts, retro objets d'art and 'frivolities'. Have your picture taken with your purchase and star on Facebook. *Rua S. Cristóvão 3 (opp. church) | http://www.facebook.com/ALoja.Lisboa | Metro (green) Rossio*

MADEIRA HOUSE (131 D5) (𝄞 M9)
Discover the famous handicrafts from Madeira, including a good selection of cork items. *Rua Augusta 131 | www.madeira-house.com | Metro (blue, green) Baixa-Chiado*

OMLET (130 C5) (𝄞 M9)
Hidden away in a Chiado courtyard, this friendly boutique sells fun souvenirs, jewellery made from angling equipment, cool bags and textiles. Closed weekends. *Calça-*

da Nova de São Francisco 10 | www.omlet.pt | Metro (blue, green) Baixa-Chiado*

PALÁCIO DO PAPEL (130 C5) (𝄞 L9)
Paul Auster's novel Oracle Night made the small blue notebook used by its protagonist trendy; today, the 'Paper Palace' (Papelaria do Calhariz) offers a good selection of the *cadernos portugueses* as pretty souvenirs for readers and writers back home. *Largo do Calhariz | Metro (blue, green) Baixa-Chiado*

SANTOS OFÍCIOS (131 D5) (𝄞 N9)
Sells traditional Portuguese crafts from all parts of the country – pottery, woollen goods, azulejos, jewellery and toys. *Rua da Madalena 87 | www.santosoficios-artesanato.pt | Eléctrico 28 to Sé*

A VIDA PORTUGUESA ★ (130 C5) (𝄞 M9)
For everybody who loves to browse, this is where you'll find a tasteful and colourful assortment of retro household products as well as stationery, cosmetics and unusual foods such as olive oil tasting sets. Everything is *made in Portugal. Rua Anchieta 11 | www.avidaportuguesa.com | Metro (blue, green) Baixa-Chiado*

TREVO (120 C3) (𝄞 O)
This shop specialises in *Arraiolos* carpets, including made-to-order. *Arraiolos* is the name for a type of cross-stitch with one long and one short stitch, lending the carpet more weight. *Av. Óscar M. Torres 33A | www.arraiolostrevo.com | Metro (yellow) Campo Pequeno*

MARKETS

FEIRA DA LADRA ★ (131 F3–4) (𝄞 O8–9)
Tuesdays and Saturdays (9am–6pm), the *Campo de Santa Clara*, to the left be-

hind the church of *São Vicente,* hosts the *Feira da Ladra,* the 'Market of the Thieving Woman' (it used to be the place to sell stolen goods). Today, it's a regular flea market selling a lot of things that might otherwise have landed on the tip. The stalls further on have better prices. But don't get your hopes up too much:

MERCADO DA RIBEIRA
(130 B–C6) (*ℳ L10*)

This spacious market hall built in the port area in 1902 shows neo-Moorish influences. This is where the farmers from outer Lisbon sell their products. There is an organic outlet too, and at the weekends there's an afternoon dancing ses-

Hunting for bargains on the 'Market of the Thieving Woman'

the professionals know exactly what to charge! *Eléctrico 28 to Voz Operário*

INSIDER TIP MERCADO CAMPO DE OURIQUE (125 D–E6) (*ℳ H–J8*)

The popular busy market in this upmarket, family-friendly and untouristy neighbourhood has an excellent selection of fresh produce, especially fruit and veg, meat and fish. The pastelaria at the corner *(Rua Coelho da Rocha 99)* claims to make the 'best chocolate cake in the world', with either dark or milk chocolate *(www.omelhorbolodechocolatedomundo.com). It's* a favourite if you find yourself invited to a Lisbon dinner. *Mon–Sat 7am–2pm | Rua Coelho da Rocha | eléctrico 28 to Rua Saraiva Carvalho*

sion to Portuguese hits. The first floor has a large room devoted to crafts. *Sun–Thu 10am–7pm, Fri/Sat 10am–10pm, market Tue–Sat 5am–2pm | Av. 24 de Julho | www.espacoribeira.pt | Metro (green) Cais do Sodré*

FASHION & ACCESSORIES

The main shopping areas are the *Baixa* with its many old-fashioned shops and the more upmarket *Chiado.* International designers have set up shop mainly along *Avenida da Liberdade,* while club and streetwear can be found in the *Bairro Alto.* Information on the Portuguese top designers: *www.modalisboa.pt*

Minuscule gloves shop: Luvaria Ulísses

ANA SALAZAR MODA

The collections of the Grande Dame of the Portuguese fashion scene, Ana Salazar, are presented in two stores. *www.anasa lazar.pt | Av. de Roma, 16* (121 D3) (*∅ O*) *| Metro (green) Roma* and – more central – *Rua do Carmo, 87* (131 D4–5) (*∅ M9*) *| Metro (green) Rossio*

CHAPELARIA AZEVEDO
(131 D4) (*∅ M9*)

This traditional hat-maker has been around since 1886. It sells hats and caps of all kinds, including made-to-measure. *Praça D. Pedro (Rossio) 69 | Metro (green) Rossio*

FÁTIMA LOPES

No one shows more skin. The famous designer from Madeira designs sexy haute couture for men and women. *www.fatimalopes.com | Rua da Ata-*

laia 36 (130 C4) (*∅ L9*) *| Metro (blue, green) Baixa-Chiado | Av. da Roma 44 D/E* (120–121 C–D2) (*∅ O*) *| Metro (green) Roma*

FLY LONDON (130 B2) (*∅ L8*)

Fly London's comfortable wedge shoes are useful for pounding Lisbon's steep pavements – the death of many a kitten heel – in style. Flagship store. *Av. da Liberdade 230 | www. flylondon.com | Metro (blue) Avenida*

JOSÉ ANTÓNIO TENENTE
(130 C5) (*∅ M9*)

In a way, Tenente is Portugal's Escada. The versatile designer has two signature fashion lines – classics and jeans – but also makes bags, pens, glasses and even skiwear. *Travessa do Carmo 8 | www.jose antoniotenente.com | Metro (blue, green) Baixa-Chiado*

INSIDER TIP ▸ LUVARIA ULÍSSES
(131 D5) (*∅ M9*)

This Lilliputian shop sells all kinds of gloves, and will also make your very own made-to-measure pair. *Rua do Carmo 87 | Metro (green) Rossio*

ROSA E TEIXEIRA (130 B–C2) (*∅ L8*)

This elegant menswear store is a Lisbon classic. Sells international designers such as Valentino and Ferragamo and its own in-house label. *Av. Liberdade 204 | www. rosaeteixeira.pt | Metro (blue) Avenida*

INSIDER TIP ▸ STIVALI STOCKSHOP
(130 C2) (*∅ L7*)

This cut-price designer outlet offers mainly women's clothing and shoes. Items from last season, by Armani, Chanel or Gucci, half-price or even cheaper. *Mon-Sat 10am–7pm | Rua Rodrigues Sampaio 19 c | www.stivali.pt | Metro (blue) Avenida*

STORYTAILORS (130 C5) (𝄞 M10)

This hip Portuguese label specialises in dramatic clothes with a hint of romance. Its clothes aim to tell a story, hence the tailor/teller pun. *Mon–Sat noon–8pm | Calçada do Ferragial 8 | www.storytailors. pt | tram 28, Metro (green) Cais do Sodré or (blue, green) Baixa-Chiado*

ZILIAN (120 A5) (𝄞 K6)

At this mecca for shoe lovers, you're sure to find something that matches that outfit from its 4500 pairs, sorted by current colour trends. Prices are reasonable. *Mon–Sat 10am–8pm | Av. António Augusto de Aguiar, 29 D (next to the El Corte Inglés department store) | www.zilian choose.com | Metro (blue) São Sebastião*

JEWELLERY

ELÓI DE JESUS (130 C5) (𝄞 M9)

Specialises in silver jewellery, including very pretty filigree work. *Rua Garrett 45 | Metro (blue, green) Baixa-Chiado*

LINHA AÉREA (131 D4) (𝄞 M9)

This is a treasure trove for style-conscious accessories junkies with small budgets. Costume jewellery, retro sunglasses, hair clips from the 1940s, toe rings and piercings are all here. *Behind Rossio/corner Rua do Carmo, Rua 1º Dezembro 3 | Metro (green) Rossio*

OURIVESARIA ALIANÇA (130 C5) (𝄞 M9)

The shop itself is worth seeing in its own right. Holds occasional exhibitions. *Rua Garrett 50 | Metro (blue, green) Baix-Chiado*

WINE & PORT WINE

CASA MACÁRIO (131 D4) (𝄞 M9)

Dependable aged port wines, gourmet products, and coffee from São Tomé are sold in an old-fashioned ambience. *Rua Augusta 272 | www.casa macario.com | Metro (green) Rossio*

SOLAR DO VINHO DO PORTO ★ ● (130 C4) (𝄞 L–M9)

This long-established tasting parlour, restyled in 2011, offers a huge range of port wine to taste and buy. *Mon–Sat 11am–midnight | Rua de São Pedro de Alcântara 45 | www.ivp.pt | Metro (blue) Restauradores, then Elevador da Glória | Metro (blue, green) Baixa-Chiado*

INSIDER TIP ● OS GOLIARDOS (130 B3) (𝄞 L8)

Okay, so this small wine store run by a young Portuguese-French couple is only open Thu–Sat evenings, but here you'll be among lisboetas rather than tourists. It sells an interesting selection of wine from producers who are individually known to the owners. It also runs wine appreciation classes, some of which include dinner. *Thu–Sat 7pm–2am | Rua da Mãe d'Água 9 | www.osgoliardos.com | Metro (blue) Avenida*

Wines by the basket at Solar do Vinho do Porto

ENTERTAINMENT

🏙 WHERE TO START?

The city's party mile, with countless bars and hangouts, is the **Bairro Alto** (Upper Town). Later at night, the action moves down the hill to **Cais do Sodré** on the Tagus shore, and further west to the **Docas** (docks) **de Alcântara** and **de Santo Amaro**. Much of **Santos**, around Avenida D. Carlos I, is given over to the teen scene, with cheap restaurants, bars and clubs.

The Portuguese capital has something for everybody: intimate fado places, live music bars with African or Brazilian rhythms, cosy pubs, chic bars and exciting clubs.

The biggest street party every evening, apart from the beginning of the week, traditionally begins in *Bairro Alto*. A crowd of mainly 20- and 30-somethings moves from bar to bar, sipping beer or a variation of the rum-based caipirinha cocktail, spilling on to the pavements, meeting old friends and making new ones. The fresh pastries baked by the **INSIDER TIP** *padaria* (bakery) in *Rua da Rosa 186,* which starts work around 1am, sell like the proverbial hot cakes. An hour later, as the bars in Bairro Alto start to close (they are subject to a 2am curfew), the exodus starts downhill to the neighbouring port district of *Cais do Sodré,* which has been transformed from a seedy area of sailors' strip bars to a trendy entertainment area with

**Night owls will be in heaven here:
on the Tagus, entertainment starts
late and offers far more than fado**

slick clubs and bars. Other popular destinations include the area around Santa Apolónia train station where *Lux is still one of the hippest clubs in town;* the *Avenida 24 Julho;* the ⭐ *Docas (Doca de Santo Amaro* and *Doca de Alcântara,* an open-air strip of restaurants and bars that also sees some daytime traffic on account of its riverside location. At weekends and on evenings preceding public holidays, the main nightlife areas are connected by **INSIDER TIP** free shuttle buses (Night Bus), though taxis are not

expensive, especially if you are travelling in a group.

Major rock and pop concerts and opera are staged at the *Coliseu (Rua das Portas de Santo Antão, 96 | www.coliseulisboa. com)* and the *Pavilhão Atlântico* at Parque das Nações *(www.pavilhaoat-lantico.pt).* For an overview of what's on, consult the bilingual *Follow me* brochure, distributed through the turismos and in many restaurants and bars; it is also published online. Tickets for all events can be bought at the central *ABEP* kiosk

BARS

at Restauradores, at *fnac* in the Chiado shopping centre and online: *www.ticketline.pt* and *www.plateia.pt*.

BARS

INSIDER TIP PENSÃO AMOR ★
(130 C5) (𝄞 M10)

The kitsch-erotic paintings on the wall are a reminder of this establishment's previous life as a hotel-brothel that used

Belo | www.myspace.com/bicaense | eléctrico 28 to Calhariz (Bica), Metro (blue, green) Baixa-Chiado

KUTA-BAR (131 F5) (𝄞 O9)

A cosy cocktail bar and lounge restaurant within the ancient walls of Alfama. *Wed–Sun from 10am, Sun brunch 11am–6pm | Travessa do Chafariz d'El Rey, 8 | www.kuta-bar.com | bus 794 to Alfândega, Metro (blue) Santa Apolónia*

Nostalgic, kitschy and very popular: the Pavilhão Chinês bar

to charge by the hour. It has been turned into a bar with a sex-shop, an origami store and a dance floor. Prices are steep, and it is usually heaving. *Daily noon–4am | Rua do Alecrim 19 | https://www.facebook.com/pensaoamor | Metro (green) Cais de Sodré*

BICAENSE (130 B–C5) (𝄞 L9)

This small bar/club hugging the rails of the *Elevador da Bica* is a favourite with Lisbon's young art scene. It puts on occasional concerts and exhibitions, and has a very popular jazz session on Wednesdays. *Closed Sun/Mon | Rua Bica Duarte*

LOUNGE (130 B5) (𝄞 L10)

This laid-back club offers fine electronic music and has a welcoming vibe. It is also very smoky. *Closed Mon | Rua da Moeda 1 | opposite the lower station of the Elevador da Bica | Eléctrico 25 to Rua S. Paulo (Bica)*

MAHJONG (130 C5) (𝄞 L9)

Done out in an eccentric Oriental look, this bar has cult status, attracting an arty crowd of theatre folk and art students. Offers table football, too, for a laugh. *Bairro Alto | Rua da Atalaia 3 | Metro (blue, green) Baixa-Chiado*

MARIA CAXUXA (130 C5) (*L9*)

This hip yet laid-back bar with jazzy electronic music is usually jam-packed, with crowds outside the door. *Mon–Sat 5pm–2am, Sun 9pm–2am | Rua da Barroca, 6–12 | eléctrico 28 to Calhariz (Bica)*

PAVILHÃO CHINÊS ⭐

(130 B4) (*L8*)

In this retro bar, bric-a-brac, kitsch and collectibles line every inch of the walls. There's also a billiards table. Tea, cakes and snacks are served as well as alcohol, all with the same old-school service. It's a must for all fans of vintage, but not cheap. *Tue–Sat from 6pm, Sun from 9pm | Rua Dom Pedro V 89 | www.bar-pavilhaochines.blogspot.com | bus 58 to Príncipe Real*

LUX ⭐ ☀ (132 C6) (*P9*)

The coolest club in town maintains its position as the hipsters' choice. The co-owner of this temple of dance is actor John Malkovich. While conversations are just about possible in the extensive first-floor lounge, in the basement the beat doesn't go much below 120 *beats per minute*. The cherry on the cake is the huge roof terrace with its great views over the Old Town and the Tagus. Up-and-coming dance bands often play gigs here, on Thursdays in particular. Expect long queues at weekends, when there's door policy from 2am. *Thu–Sat 11pm–6am | Avenida Infante D. Henrique | Cais da Pedra opposite Santa Apolónia railway station | www.luxfragil.com | Metro (blue) Santa Apolónia*

CLUBS

B.LEZA (130 B6) (*L10*)

Meet Lisbon's African community. A lot of live music is played in this spacious venue, especially Cape Verdean and Angolan – morna, funaná and kizomba. Expect hot rhythms into the small hours. *Wed–Sun 10.30pm-4am | Cais da Ribeira | https://sites.google.com/site/blezaacr/programa | Metro (green) Cais do Sodré*

FRÁGIL (130 C4) (*L9*)

This is a fixture on the dance circuit, with techno and disco sounds mixed by international DJs. At weekends, this small club is packed. *Tue–Sat 11.30pm–4am | Rua da Atalaia 126 | www.fragil.com.pt | Metro (blue, green) Baixa-Chiado*

INCÓGNITO (129 F3) (*K9*)

Timelessly trendy, this small club serves an excellent blend of rock and Brit pop. *Closed Sun–Tue | Rua Poiais de São Bento 37 | www.incognitobar.com | Eléctrico 28 to Calçada Combro*

⭐ **Docas**
On the boardwalk: open-air restaurants and bars → p. 75

⭐ **Pensão Amor**
Bar of the moment, with that special touch → p. 76

⭐ **Pavilhão Chinês**
For lovers of all things retro-kitsch → p. 77

⭐ **Lux**
Still the undisputed meeting point for hipsters → p. 77

⭐ **Mesa de Frades**
Intimate fado experience, surrounded by top-to-bottom azulejos → p. 79

⭐ **Musicbox**
Laid-back concerts from avant-garde to mainstream → p. 80

MARCO POLO HIGHLIGHTS

FADO

INSIDER TIP **OP ART** (128 B6) *(𝓜 G11)*
With its unusual location — the small glass pavilion is situated on the outer quay of the Santo Amaro docks — this club is slightly off the bar mile. In the Real neighbourhood, in the heart of the gay community. *Fri/Sat 11.40pm–6am | Rua da Imprensa Nacional 104 B | tel. 9 63 16 06 02 | www.trumps.pt | Metro (yellow) Rato*

Lounging and dancing in the coolest club in town, the legendary Lux

daytime, you can enjoy a relaxed meal with a great view over the Tagus; from 3am, electro, techno and house music prevail. Hard-core dancers will be happy here! *Closed Mon | Pontão das Docas de Santo Amaro | www.opartcafe.com | eléctrico 15, 18 to Av. Infante Santo*

ROTERDÃO (130 C5–6) *(𝓜 M10)*
The former doorman of the *Incógnito,* called *D'Artagnan* by those in the know, has revamped one of the strip clubs in the old port quarter, turning the slightly dodgy 'Rotterdam' into a new meeting point. Expect music from the '70s to the '90s, plus timeless classics. *Daily 2pm–4am | Rua Nova de Carvalho 28 | Metro (green) Cais do Sodré*

TRUMPS (130 A3) *(𝓜 K8)*
A classic disco on Lisbon's gay scene, yet very hetero-friendly too. Its drag show has even veterans blushing. In the Principe

FADO

● Many fado venues cater primarily to tourists, offering professional fado that lacks the edge of the real thing. Finding pure fado is really a matter of luck. Usually there is no entrance charge, but food and drink are considerably more expensive than in regular restaurants. A bottle of wine costs at least 20 euros. Those arriving late (from 11pm at the earliest) can escape the otherwise obligatory meal. Look out for signs announcing *fado vadio:* amateur fado, where anybody can have a go – within limits, this is not karaoke!

CLUBE DE FADO (131 E5) *(𝓜 N10)*
This high-standard if fairly touristy fado restaurant within the historic walls has a warm atmosphere. Book ahead. *Daily | Rua de S. João da Praça 94 | tel. 2 18 85 27 04 | www.clube-de-fado.com | eléctrico 28 to Sé*

MESA DE FRADES ★ (131 F4) (*Ø O9*)

You'll be mingling with the younger generation at this beautiful fado tavern in a former chapel. It isn't overly expensive, and its menu always includes a vegetarian dish of the day. Reservations are recommended. *Closed Tue | Rua dos Remédios, 139 A | tel. 9 17 02 94 36 | Metro (blue) Santa Apolónia*

A NINI (125 F3) (*Ø K6*)

At Nini's INSIDER TIP regular fado sessions on a Thursday night, fado singers meet fado experts. It offers an authentic experience and Portuguese cuisine. *Thu from 9pm, fado from around 11pm (booking advised) | tel. 2 13 87 00 41 | Rua D. Francisco Manuel de Melo 36-A | bus 12 to Rua Artilharia Um/Rua D. Francisco M. Melo*

PARREIRINHA DE ALFAMA (131 F5) (*Ø O9*)

This popular fado restaurant is owned by Argentina Santos, a legend of Lisbon fado, who can sometimes be persuaded to perform. *Closed Sun | Beco do Espírito Santo 1 | on Largo Chafariz de Dentro | tel. 2 18 86 82 09 | bus 28 to Casa Conto*

SENHOR VINHO (129 E3) (*Ø K9*)

This renowned fado venue in the Madragoa part of town is owned by Maria da Fé, another big name in fado. Those who want to catch the lady herself should telephone around 6pm to see if she will be performing. Reservations recommended. *Daily 7.30pm–2am, fado from 9pm | Rua do Meio à Lapa 18 | tel. 2 13 97 26 81 | www.srvinho.com | eléctrico 25 bis Rua Santana à Lapa*

TASCA DO CHICO (130 C4) (*Ø L–M9*)

Sometimes real fado feeling emerges from this cosy little *tasca* in the heart of the Bairro Alto. INSIDER TIP Mondays and Wednesdays fado vadio. There is an Alfama branch too. *Daily | Rua Diário de Notícias 39 | tel. 9 65 05 96 70 | http:// www.facebook.com/pages/Tasca-do-Chico/139580167791 | eléctrico 28 to Praça Luis Camões*

CINEMAS

Foreign films are shown in the original version with Portuguese subtitles. Current blockbusters are screened in the shopping centre cinemas. Tickets are cheaper than in most European capitals, and many cinemas offer a 50 per cent discount on Monday. To view the schedule, check the daily newspapers, such as *Diário de Notícias* or *Público* or *www. cinecartaz.publico.pt*

INSIDER TIP CINEMATECA (130 B2) (*Ø L8*)

This place is heaven for film addicts on a low budget (ticket only 2.50 euros), and there is a cinema museum *(Mon–Fri 2pm–9.30pm, free admission)*, exhibitions, library and a cinema bookshop too. Two rooms show international art-house cinema. There is also a good café restau-

Live performance in a small fado restaurant

rant with a pretty terrace. *Closed Sun | Rua Barata Salgueiro 39 | www.cinemateca.pt | Metro(blue) Avenida*

ARTS CENTRES

BRAÇO DE PRATA (O) (*⌘ O*)
Music, performance art and dance workshops take place in this former ammunition factory. It has a welcoming café, and the place is full of books. It is slightly outside the city centre, so grab a cab. *Rua da Fábrica do Material de Guerra 1 | tel. 9 65 51 80 68 | www.bracodeprata.net | train Braço de Prata (from Entrecampos or Oriente)*, bus 28, 783

CENTRO CULTURAL DE BELÉM
(126 B5) (*⌘ C12*)
Stages opera, classical, jazz, international pop, rock and ethno music, ballet, modern dance and exhibitions. *Tel. 213 61 24 44 | www.ccb.pt | train from Cais do Sodré, eléctrico 15 to Centro Cultural de Belém*

LOW BUDGET

▶ To top it all, Lisbon's nightlife is not only vibrant, it's cheap too. A small beer on a *Bairro Alto* street might set you back as little as 1 euro; a half-litre 'bucket' of caipirinha about a fiver.

▶ To ensure that the clubs are full on weekdays as well as weekends, women get free drinks in a number of places. Ladies' nights are very popular with the gentlemen too. *Tue at Dock's (Doca da Alcântara) | Wed at Plateau* ((129 E4) (*⌘ K10*) *Escadinhas da Praia, 7 | Santos) and at the W Club* ((128 B4–5) (*⌘ G10*) *Rua Maria Luísa Holstein, 13).*

LX FACTORY ● (128 B4) (*⌘ G10*)
This hip arts complex with designer workshops occupies a former textile factory. The cool *Ler Devagar* bookshop-cum-café has books up to the ceiling, a liberal smoking policy and holds experimental concerts on the upper floor. It stays open until 2am. There are clubs, restaurants, and a convivial pizzeria too. *Daily, varying opening times | Rua Rodrigues Faria 103 | tel. 2 13 14 33 99 | www.lxfactory.com | eléctrico 15 E, 18 E to Calvário*

MUSIC CLUBS & LIVE EVENTS

FORA DA MODA (131 E5) (*⌘ N9*)
A cosy and welcoming new spot to experience varied live music in Alfama. Next to San Estêvão church. *Wed–Sun 6pm–4am | Largo de S. Estêvão 9 | Metro (blue) Santa Apolonia, then 10 mins on foot*

HOT CLUBE (130 C3) (*⌘ L8*)
This meeting point for jazz lovers was destroyed by fire in 2009, but has resumed operations one door along. Tue/Wed jam sessions. *Closed Sun–Mon | Praça da Alegria 39 | www.hotclubedeportugal. org | Metro (yellow) Avenida*

MUSICBOX ★ (130 C5–6) (*⌘ M10*)
This tunnel-like, yet well-aired, club is a fixture for all fans of house, electro pop and alternative sounds. Nothing happens here before 2am unless it's a concert day. *Tue/Wed 10pm–4am, Thu to Sat 11pm–7am | Rua Nova de Carvalho, 24 | www.musicboxlisboa.com | Metro (green) Cais do Sodré*

RITZ CLUBE (130 C3) (*⌘ M8*)
This legendary dancehall reopened in 2012. *Sun–Wed 10pm-4am, Thu–Sat till 6am; closed Mon | Rua da Glória 57 | tel. 21 241 7604 | www.ritzclube.com | Metro (blue) Restauradores or Avenida*

PUB CRAWL

WILDWALKERS (130 C5) (*M9*)
'3 bars, 4 shots, 2 beers, 1 club': well, if that doesn't get you in the swing of things… Six times a week, this pub crawl with Portuguese party guides takes place in Bairro Alto. Every Thursday, the Wildwalkers also run a fado evening. The tours attract a young crowd and offer a good-value first-time overview. *Meeting Mon–Sat 10.30pm at Largo Luis de Camões | tel. 910489724 | www.wild walkers.eu | Metro (blue, green) Baixa-Chiado*

THEATRE, MUSICAL & OPERA

Lisbon's long-established theatres, such as *São Luíz, Trindade* in Chiado and *Dona Maria II* on Rossio, are beautiful to behold, but performances are in Portuguese only. The *São Carlos* opera mostly puts on Italian works. The Gulbenkian Foundation has its own concert hall and orchestra: *www.musica.gulbenkian.pt.* Tickets: 10–60 euros.

INSIDER TIP **TEATRO DO BAIRRO**
(130 C4) (*L9*)
New in 2011, this Bairro Alto venue offers a changing programme of arts events, including plays, fado, contemporary dance, films and Cape Verdean dance music. *Opening times change, depending on the schedule | Rua Luz Soriano 63 | tel. 213473358 or 913211263 | www. teatrodobairro.org | Metro (blue, green) Baixa-Chiado, then 15 min on foot*

TEATRO CAMÕES (117 F4) (*S3*)
Following the Expo, the national ballet troupe *Companhia Nacional de Bailado (CNB)* moved in here; the theatre receives visiting ballet companies too. *Parque das Nações, Passeio do Neptuno |*

tel. 218923477 | www.cnb.pt | Metro (red) Oriente

TEATRO NACIONAL DE SÃO CARLOS (130 C5) (*M10*)
Even those not interested in opera should try to see the grand entrance and the paintings in the auditorium. *Largo de São Carlos | tel. 213253045 | www.saocarlos.pt | Metro (blue, green) Baixa-Chiado*

Musical hits at the Teatro Politeama

TEATRO POLITEAMA (130 C3) (*M8*)
INSIDER TIP In-house director Filipe La Féria puts on all manner of musicals – international musicals Portuguese-style and Portuguese originals such as a musical about fado queen Amália Rodrigues. *Tue–Sat 9.30, Sat/Sun also at 5pm | Rua Portas de Santo Antão 109 | tel. 213245500 | www.teatropo liteama. net | Metro (blue) Restauradores*

WHERE TO STAY

Lisbon has over 35,000 tourist beds, yet in high season demand can exceed supply. In June in particular, when Lisbon is one big festival, an early reservation is highly recommended.

The city's hotels are classified into five categories, following international standards. Most of the international chains are in the side streets and avenidas around the *Praça Marquês de Pombal*. For comfortable accommodation with a bit more character, check out the *estalagens* and *albergarias*; in terms of price, they are equivalent to a four- or five-star hotel. Relatively cheap accommodation is available in pensions *(pensão)* and residences *(residencial)*. A new phenomenon in Lisbon is the backpacker hostels that have come in on the back of the low-budget flights. At the 'Hoscars', awarded to the best hostels worldwide, Lisbon has held the title of the world's best hostel city for several years. Winning establishments in 2011 were *Travellers House* and *Lisbon Lounge (see p. 88)*. Twin rooms with two separate beds are usually larger and a bit more expensive than double rooms *(duplo)*. A single room is a *quarto individual*.

HOTELS: EXPENSIVE

ALTIS BELÉM HOTEL & SPA
(126 B6) (∅ C12)

The latest smart hotel in town has a fabulous location overlooking the Tagus in Belém. State-of-the art design, a great spa, and an award-winning restaurant. *50 rooms | Doca do Bom Sucesso |*

Lisbon has accommodation to suit any budget: from hostels and pensions with Old Town flair to world-class luxury hotels

tel. 2 10 40 02 00 | www.altishotels.com | Eléctrico 15 to CCB

AS JANELAS VERDES (129 E4) *(⏸ J10)*
The hotel 'of the green windows' is housed in an 18th-century palace near the *Museu de Arte Antiga*. The rooms are comfortable and sunny, while the romantic garden and the library terrace are perfect spots for relaxing. *29 rooms | Rua das Janelas Verdes 47 | tel. 2 13 96 81 43 | www.asjanelasverdes.com | bus 727 to Rua das Janelas Verdes*

BAIRRO ALTO HOTEL ☀ (130 C5) *(⏸ M9)*
Luxury with Old Town character: staying at this small boutique hotel you'll feel like a true lisboeta, right in the heart of the hustle and bustle, but with all the comforts and service of a top hotel. The unbeatable – even though coffee prices are up there with the Uffizi in Florence – **INSIDER TIP** terrace bar is open to non-residents *(in summer daily 12.30–midnight). 55 rooms | Praça Luis de Camões 2 | tel. 2 13 40 82 88 | www.bairroaltohotel. com | Metro (blue, green) Baixa-Chiado*

HOTEL BRITÂNIA (130 C2) (* L8*)

This renovated art-deco gem offers generous rooms with plenty of atmosphere. Marble baths, formal service, and some eco touches. The only downside is its view onto an office block. *32 rooms | Rua Rodrigues Sampaio 17 | tel. 2 13 15 50 16 | www. hotel-britania.com | Metro (blue) Avenida*

LISBOA PLAZA (130 C3) (*L8*)

This centrally located hotel belongs to the Heritage group, which specialises in hotéis de charme. It's pretty, cosy and has plenty of atmosphere. *94 rooms, 12 suites | Travessa Salitre/Av da Liberdade | tel. 2 13 21 82 18 | www.lisbonplazahotel. com | Metro (blue) Avenida*

Lisboa Regency Chiado: rooms in modern colonial style, many with private balcony or terrace

FONTANA DESIGN HOTEL
(120 C6) (*M6*)

Not quite as central as the competition, but it offers clean, minimalist design in black and white and every comfort at relatively low prices. Two restaurants: one Japanese (INSIDER TIP Sa Sushi workshop), the other Portuguese-Mediterranean. *139 rooms/suites | Rua Eng. Vieira da Silva 2 | tel. 2 10 41 06 00 | www.fontanaparkhotel.com | Metro (yellow) Picoas*

INTERNACIONAL DESIGN HOTEL
(131 D4) (*M9*)

This new hotel with its pretty purple-and-white Belle Époque façade is situated right on Rossio. Each floor has a trendy design theme: Zen, Pop, Urban, and Tribal. Room sizes range from small to extra-large. Fine restaurant, good service. *55 rooms | Rua da Betesga, 3 | tel. 2 13 24 09 90 | www.idesignhotel.com | Metro (green) Rossio*

LISBOA REGENCY CHIADO ★ ⋇
(130–131 C–D5) (*M9*)

Tastefully renovated establishment in the heart of Chiado. The best rooms have their own terrace. Even non-residents, however, can enjoy the INSIDER TIP wonderful view from the terrace of the *Bar Entretanto* on the seventh floor (daily noon–midnight, with free Wi-Fi). *Armazéns do Chiado | Rua Nova de Almada 114 | tel. 2 13 25 61 00 | www.lisboaregencychiado. com | Metro (blue, green) Baixa-Chiado*

MARQUÊS DE POMBAL ⋇
(130 B2) (*L7*)

Contemporary and stylish hotel, with cosy, quiet rooms and fine views across Lisbon's splendid central boulevard. Very friendly staff. *123 rooms | Av. da Liberdade 243 | tel. 2 13 19 79 00 | www.hotel-marquesdepombal.pt | Metro (blue, yellow) Marquês de Pombal*

SOLAR DO CASTELO ⭐

(131 E4) (*∅ N9*)

This delightful, cosy hotel nestles within the walls of the Castelo de São Jorge. The 18th-century palace has been tastefully restored, and the buffet breakfast is taken in the attractive courtyard. *14 rooms | Rua das Cozinhas 2 | tel. 2 18 80 60 50 | www. solardocastelo.com | bus 37 to Castelo*

HOTEL TIVOLI JARDIM

(130 B2–3) (*∅ L8*)

Offers pleasant ambience and good service, but the main draws are the INSIDER TIP heated pool in the garden and the new Sky Bar. Central location. You might want to stay away from the ground-floor rooms at the back. *119 rooms | Rua Júlio César Machado 7–9 | tel. 2 13 59 10 00 | www.tivolihotels.com | Metro (blue) Avenida*

YORK HOUSE ⭐ (129 E4) (*∅ J10*)

Charming boutique hotel in a former convent in Lapa. The rooms are classically modern with views on to the romantic patio. *32 rooms | Rua das Janelas Verdes 32 | tel. 2 13 96 24 35 | www.yorkhouselisboa. com | bus 727 to Rua das Janelas Verdes*

HOTELS: MODERATE

CASA DE SÃO MAMEDE

(130 A3) (*∅ K8*)

This quiet, small family hotel in a pretty 18th-century town palace enjoys a central location for Bairro Alto and Chiado. *28 rooms | Rua da Escola Politécnica 159 | tel. 2 13 96 31 66 | www.saomamede.web. pt | Metro (yellow) Rato*

NH LIBERDADE ⭐ ☼

(130 C3) (*∅ L8*)

A modern feel-good hotel providing top service in an equally top location. Stylish and contemporary, it has stunning views

from the rooftop pool. Some rooms have a private terrace. *83 rooms | Av da Liberdade 180 B | tel. 2 13 51 40 60 | www.nh-hotels.com | Metro (blue) Avenida*

HOTEL OLISSIPPO CASTELO ☼

(131 E4) (*∅ N9*)

This hotel hugs the lower walls of the Castelo São Jorge. The comfortable rooms are equipped with marble bathrooms, and there are fine views of the city from nearly all the rooms; some have their own terrace. *24 rooms | R. Costa do Castelo 126 | tel. 2 18 82 01 90, reservations: 2 13 18 27 90 | www.hotelolis sippocastelo.com | eléctrico 12 to S. Tomé*

RIBEIRA TEJO ☼ (130 C5) (*∅ L10*)

Opened in 2011, this stylish boutique guesthouse behind the market hall is ideal for the nightlife around Cais do Sodré (don't worry, the windows have double-glazing!), for Tagus river cruises and trains

---

⭐ **Lisboa Regency Chiado**
Oriental touches, unique views
→ p. 84

⭐ **Solar do Castelo**
Romantic hotel on the castle mound → p. 85

⭐ **York House**
In a former convent, with period furniture and French cuisine
→ p. 85

⭐ **NH Liberdade**
Unobtrusively chic and a top location → p. 85

⭐ **Travellers House**
Proud bearer of the title 'Best Hostel in the World' → p. 88

MARCO POLO HIGHLIGHTS

to the beach. A river view is on offer from the second floor upwards. The young owners provide guests with a customised map with loads of ideas for restaurants, fado clubs, etc. *15 rooms | Travessa do São Paulo 5 | tel. 9 13 29 01 02 | www.casadobairro.pt | Metro (green) Cais do Sodré*

ALBERGARIA SENHORA DO MONTE
(131 E3) (⨊ N8)
Quiet hotel near Alfama with fine views from most rooms The supplement for rooms with a private terrace is well worth it paying. *28 rooms | Calçada do Monte, 39 | tel. 2 18 86 60 02 | www.senhoramonte.blogspot.com | eléctrico 28 to Graça*

HOTELS: BUDGET

ANJO AZUL *(130 B–C4) (⨊ L9)*
This small and charming pension is in a quiet corner of the Bairro Alto. Offers very friendly service. All rooms with private bathroom, TV, DVD, Internet con-

LUXURY HOTELS

Hotel Avenida Palace (130 C4) *(⨊ M9)*
This grand hotel is housed in a palace dating back to 1892, right on Rossio. All rooms are soundproofed and furnished in classic style. *82 rooms, doubles from 260 euros | Rua 1º de Dezembro 123 | tel. 2 13 21 81 00 | www.hotel-avenida-palace.pt | Metro (blue) Restauradores*

Lapa Palace (129 D4) *(⨊ J10)*
One of the most beautiful luxury choices in town resides in a town palace in the diplomats' quarter. Top quality and service, pool and park. *89 rooms, doubles from 355 euros | Rua do Pau da Bandeira 4 | tel. 2 13 94 94 94 | www.lapapalace.com | suburban train Santos*

Palácio Belmonte (131 E4) *(⨊ N9)*
If you don't have to think twice about paying 600 euros per night, sleep in the oldest town palace in Lisbon. If you simply want to look at what you are missing, you can approach the palace uphill on Rua dos Cegos and have a coffee in the (sadly not always open) café in the courtyard. The palace has been used as a backdrop in Wim Wenders' Lisbon Story and Mastroianni's last film Pereira Maintains. *11 suites | Pateo Dom Fradique, Encosta do Castelo | tel. 2 18 81 66 00 | www.palaciobelmonte.com | eléctrico 12E to S. Tomé*

Pestana Palace Hotel *(127 F4) (⨊ F10)*
This 19th-century palace is located on the edge of the city centre in the upmarket residential neighbourhood of Alto de Santo Amaro, with views over the Tagus estuary. The rooms are in the modern annexe. *173 rooms, doubles from 290 euros | Rua Jau 54 | tel. 2 13 61 56 00 | www.pestana. com | eléctrico 18 to Alto de Santo Amaro*

Hotel Ritz Four Seasons *(130 A1) (⨊ K7)*
This is still Number One in Lisbon. Location, views, rooms, service – all are perfect, and complemented by a fabulous spa. *284 rooms and suites, doubles from 355 euros | Rua Rodrigo da Fonseca, 88 | tel. 2 13 81 14 00 | www.fourseasons.com | Metro (blue, yellow) Marquês de Pombal*

This is the life: at the Lapa Palace hotel pool

nection and mini bar. Ask for a room on the third or fourth floor for more natural light and better views. *20 rooms | Rua Luz Soriano 75 | tel. 213 47 80 69 and 213 46 71 86 | www.anjoazul.com | eléctrico 28 to Calhariz (Bica)*

HOTEL BOTÂNICO (130 B3) (𝔐 L8)
The rooms in this central and quiet three-star hotel are simple yet cosy, and the upper floors have fine views across the city. Friendly service. *30 rooms | Rua Mãe d'Água 16–20 | tel. 213 42 03 92 | www.hotelbotanico.net | Metro (blue) Avenida*

HOTEL JORGE V (130 B2) (𝔐 L7–8)
In a side street off Avenida da Liberdade, Jorge V has comfortable rooms with satellite TV, a mini bar and safe. There is also a cosy lobby bar and the staff are obliging . *49 rooms | Rua Mouzinho da Silveira 3 | tel. 213 56 25 25 | www.hotel jorgev.com | Metro Marquês de Pombal*

PENSÃO LONDRES (130 C4) (𝔐 L8–9)
Renovated pension on the edge of the party quarter of Bairro Alto – hence the double-glazed windows. Rooms with and without a private bathroom are available; the ones that are en-suite also have air-conditioning. *40 rooms | Rua D. Pedro V 53 | tel. 213 46 22 03 | www.pensaolondres.com.pt | bus 92 to Rua Dom Pedro V*

PENSÃO NINHO DAS ÁGUIAS (131 D–E4) (𝔐 N9)
Guests stay here to experience the atmosphere of the Old Town and are happy to forego certain comforts – the spiral staircase is quite something. It is very good value, though, and quiet. Terrace. *16 rooms | Costa do Castelo 74 | tel. 218 85 40 70 | eléctrico 12 to S. Tomé*

PENSÃO PRAÇA DA FIGUEIRA (131 D4) (𝔐 M9)
Super-central, old-fashioned and well-run pension on a square right next to Rossio. Some rooms have a private bathroom; those that don't are very cheap indeed (30 euros). Most rooms can receive the free Wi-Fi signal. *31 rooms | Travessa Nova de S. Domingos 9, 3 esq. | tel. 213 42 43 23 | www.pensaopra cadafigueira.com | Metro (green) Rossio*

APARTMENTS

RESIDENCIAL DOM SANCHO
(130 C3) (*M L8*)
Small family hotel in a fine old building. Cosy rooms, air conditioning, minibar, cable TV. Personal and friendly service. *40 rooms | Av. da Liberdade 202, 2nd floor | tel. 213 51 31 60 | www.domsancho.com | Metro (blue) Avenida*

RESIDENCIAL FLORESCENTE
(130 C3) (*M M8*)
Comfortable rooms, some with a balcony, and generous dorm-style rooms too. Breakfast is served in the new in-house restaurant. *68 rooms | R. Portas de Santo Antão 99 | tel. 213 42 66 09 | www.residencialflorescente.com | Metro (blue) Restauradores*

RESIDENCIAL HORIZONTE
(120 B6) (*M L6*)
Pleasant rooms with TV and air conditioning next to the Eduardo VII city park. Friendly atmosphere. The rooms 802–805 have **INSIDER TIP** large terraces with views of the park (with no supplement). Free Wi-Fi at reception. *52 rooms | Av António Augusto de Aguiar 42 | tel. 213 53 95 26 | www.hotelhorizonte. com | Metro (blue) Parque*

SANA EXECUTIVE (120 B4) (*M L5*)
Friendly, quiet hotel with garden and pretty rooms, renovated in 2009, and only a stone's throw from the Gulbenkian Museum. *72 rooms | Av. Conde de Valbom 56 | tel. 217 95 11 57 | www.sana hotels.com | Metro (blue) São Sebastião*

SANA REX (130 A1) (*M K7*)
Alongside the out-and-out luxury hotels, this one is a good standard one level down. Classically furnished, comfortable rooms; fabulous views from the upper floors. *68 rooms | Rua Castilho 169 | tel. 213 88 21 61 | www.sanahotels.com | Metro (blue, yellow) Marquês de Pombal*

HOTEL ZENIT LISBOA (120 B5) (*M L6*)
Four-star hotel belonging to a Spanish chain. Intimate, stylish and modern. Good value for money. *86 rooms | Av. 5 de Outubro 11 | tel. 213 10 22 00 | www.zenithoteles. com | Metro (yellow) Saldanha or Picoas*

APARTMENTS

APARTHOTEL VIP EDEN
(130 C4) (*M M9*)
Functional 2 and 4-bed apartments with kitchenette, right next to Rossio. Rooftop

Central location with rooftop pool: Aparthotel VIP Eden

pool/bar. Very reasonable in the shoulder season; smokers' apartments also available. *134 apts. | Praça dos Restauradores 24 | tel. 213 21 66 00 | www.viphotels.com | Metro (blue) Restauradores*

CASA VILLA SERRA (130 C3) (Ø *M8*)
Apartments of varying sizes and styles in Pena, a central yet untouristy part of town. Your hosts, a dynamic American couple, will look after everything, and even provide a daily newsletter listing what's on in the city. Addresses are provided at booking. *Tel. 913 46 45 17 | www. visiting portugal.com/casavillaserra.htm (also /santana.htm) | Metro (blue) Restauradores or (green) Rossio*

CHIADO 16 (130–131 C–D5) (Ø *M10*)
Four fancy B & B apartments sleeping 2–4 people in upmarket Chiado. Crystal chandeliers, the ubiquitous Nespresso machine in the entrance hall, fast-speed internet. *Largo da Academia das Belas Artes 16 | tel. 213 94 16 16 | www.chiado16. com | Metro (green, blue) Baixa-Chiado*

MY HOME IN LISBON (131 E3) (Ø *N8*)
Classy apartment sleeping up to 6 people in the Graça neighbourhood; in the summer, breakfast is served in the neighbouring B & B guesthouse *(house No. 50)*. The owner also has apartments in other parts of town. *Calçada do Monte 10 | tel. 919 09 05 95 | www.micasaenlisboa.com | Eléctrico 28*

HOSTELS

Both of the classic youth hostels offer 24-hour service, common rooms, restaurant, bar and breakfast (2 euros). The youth hostel membership card can be issued on the spot, but reserve in good time. *Tel. 707 20 30 30 | www.pousadasjuventude.pt*

POUSADA DA JUVENTUDE (120 B6) (Ø *L6*)
Doubles in this pretty building from 43 euros, dorm from 15 euros per person | Rua Andrade Corvo 46 | tel. 213 53 26 96 | Metro (yellow) Picoas

POUSADA DA JUVENTUDE PARQUE DAS NAÇÕES (117 D1) (Ø *R1*)
Double 34 euros, dorm room 14 euros per person | Rua de Moscavide 47 | tel. 218 92 08 90 | Metro (red) Oriente

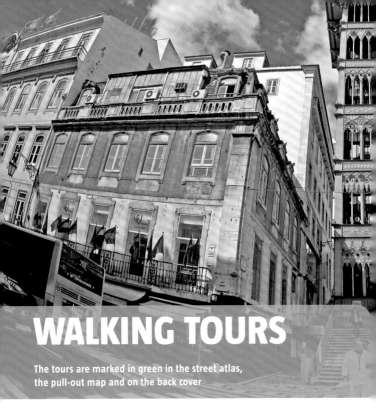

WALKING TOURS

The tours are marked in green in the street atlas,
the pull-out map and on the back cover

1 ONE DAY IN THE LISBON OF YESTERDAY AND TODAY

Belém is a friendly part of town, on the banks of the river Tagus, with carefully tended parks and gardens. Here, you will find architectural masterpieces and great museums. Once a sleepy fishing village outside the gates of the city, Belém was catapulted into the spotlight by the great Portuguese explorers, who departed from and returned from here over 500 years ago. This is the best place to come to learn about Portugal's history and culture. Schedule at least a day for Belém, and remember that on Mondays, apart from the CCB's Berardo Collection, nearly all sights are closed.

The best way to begin this tour is to catch the Eléctrico 15 from Praça do Comércio to the 'Belém' stop. If you fancy getting some exercise, use the path along the river shore *(6km/5.5mi)*. Depending on when you visit, you will see the Coach museum *(Museu Nacional dos Coches)* → p. 48 either to your right, in its current position, or already in its new home to the left. The collection of magnificent coaches and carriages ranging from the 16th to the 19th centuries is unique in the world and well worth seeing. The pink-coloured Palácio National da Ajuda next door is the seat of the Portuguese president (with museum → p. 50). If the flag is flying, the president is in. On Saturday afternoons and Sundays, guided tours through the palace and its garden

Photo: Elevador de Santa Justa

Leafy squares and lofty heights:
discover Lisbon in a maze of alleyways,
with a bird's-eye view – or on two wheels

are available *(10am–5pm | admission 5 euros)*. Every third Sunday of the month, from 11am, the Lisbon version of the Changing of the Guards takes place with suitable pomp and circumstance.

Back on Rua de Belém, the house at No. 86 contains the traditional Pastéis de Belém → p. 59 pastry shop, selling the country's famous custard tarts. The small INSIDER TIP *Caseiro* restaurant *(No. 35, closed Sun, Moderate)* is considered one of Lisbon's best fish restaurants. Behind the row of houses, the palm trees

of the Jardim Botânico rise up. This is a well-kept green oasis with fishponds and exotic plants, patrolled by parrots, peacocks and turtles *(in summer Mon–Thu 9am–6pm, Sat/Sun 11am–7pm, in winter Mon–Thu 9am–5pm, Sat/Sun 10am–5pm | admission 2 euros)*.

From here, it's only a few yards to the Praça do Império. Spreading out in front of you is the imposing Hieronymus Monastery → p. 45, not only an architectural masterpiece, but a central part of Portuguese culture and identity. In front, amidst the perfectly trimmed hedges, stone benches and statues, stands the Fonte Luminosa, a decorative fountain that is colourfully illuminated at night.

of the monument. To the west, also on the shore, is the Torre de Belém → p. 5, one of the best examples of Manueline architecture and an emblem of the

The viewing platform atop the Torre de Belém offers fine views of the Tagus

The western wing of the Hieronymite Monastery houses the Museu Nacional de Arqueologia → p. 47. Next door, the fascinating Museu de Marinha → p. 46 displays an impressive collection of model ships.

On the western side of the square is the extensive Centro Cultural de Belém → p. 80 arts centre, completed in 1992. Initially controversial, the edifice of pink-hued marble is now widely appreciated, not least because of the many excellent events that are held here. To get to the massive Monument to the Discoveries, the Padrão dos Descobrimentos → p. 49 on the shore of the Tagus, take an underpass (the entrance to which lies slightly hidden; look for the pedestrian sign). Don't miss the view of the marble mosaic from the viewing platform on top

city. Pedestrians have to detour slightly around the marina in order to get to the tower. The pedestrian footbridge crossing the railway line leads to the Largo da Princesa; from there, you can take the Eléctrico 15 back into the city centre.

2 A STROLL THROUGH THE UPPER TOWN

The *miradouros* ('golden views') are among the most beautiful that Lisbon has to offer. This stroll passes several stunning viewpoints, leads through the fancier part of the Bairro Alto and to the Chiado literary quarter: a relaxed half-day walk. The tour starts in the Lower Town at the Praça dos Restauradores → p. 38. From here, the Elevador da Glória → p. 35 transports you to the Upper Town, saving the walk. At top you'll find the magnificent viewing terrace of the Miradouro São Pedro de Alcântara → p. 42 affording fabulous views across to the castle mound of the Castelo de São Jorge → p. 29.

Continue uphill into the Rua D. Pedro V, perhaps stopping to sample a couple of typical convent pastries at 'Doce Historia' on the corner. This is the fancier part of the Bairro Alto with fine old town palaces, exclusive antiques dealers and art galleries. One eye-catcher is the art nouveau bakery Padaria São Roque (No. 57), also called Catedral do Pão (Cathedral of Bread) by lisboetas. In the friendly gourmet shop Moy (No. 111) Lisbon's yuppies do their Sunday shopping. A lovely place to chill out is the Indian-themed terrace café ● Lost In (No. 56). 'Lose' – or find? – yourself in the shade of a medlar tree, with far-reaching views across to the Castelo. There's even a couple of beds to sit on. An Indian clothes store completes the picture (Tue–Sat from 12.30, Mon from 4pm).

Only a stone's throw away, discover one of the city' lovely small parks – Príncipe Real. The massive crown of a sublime old cedar tree in its centre is supported by a cast-iron trellis, forming an extraordinary canopy. On Saturday morning a popular INSIDER TIP organic farmers' market takes place on the edge of the park.

Head downhill from here, taking the quiet Rua do Século, which is lined with pretty 17th-century buildings. Standing at the corner with Rua da Academia das Ciências, the Palácio Pombal, with its graceful archway, was the birthplace of the great figure of Lisbon's urban renewal. Hiding behind house No. 123 is the Carmelite Convento dos Cardães (Mon–Sat 2.30–5.30pm / admission 2 euros), a Baroque gem. The gilded woodcarvings at the splendid altar and the azulejos are worth seeing.

At the end of the street, head briefly uphill, to the left along Calçada do Combro and then right through the Rua Marechal Saldanha to the Miradouro de Santa Catarina → p. 41. From here, far-reaching views over the Tagus open up, with the Ponte 25 de Abril → p. 54 and the striking Cristo Rei statue → p. 51 on the other side of the river. The Noobai Café ✳ (daily from noon / www.noobai cafe.com) clings to the Miradouro like a bird's nest (it is entered via the rooftop). Fresh juices, salads and sandwiches with intriguing fillings can be enjoyed along with the stunning views.

Back in the Calçada do Combro, the walk continues uphill in the direction of Chiado, past the top terminus of the quaint Elevador da Bica → p. 40 and the fine square commemorating the national poet, the Largo de Camões. Two Baroque churches flank the square. On the northern side, stands the Igreja do Loreto with its flight of steps; opposite is the Igreja da Encarnação, whose ceiling paintings have recently been beautifully restored. There is always a bustle around Chiado. The terraces of two long-established traditional cafés A Brasileira → p. 58 and Benard (closed Sun) with its wonderful croissants, offer an opportunity to sit down for a breather. There is a lot to explore around here. Rua Serpa Pinto leads downhill past the opera house São Carlos (which has an elegant bistro) to the Museu do Chiado → p. 42, for excellent contemporary art exhibitions. Going down Rua Garrett instead and taking a left down into Rua do Carmo, you will reach the Elevador de Santa Justa → p. 35. Take the elevator back into the Upper Town and enjoy stunning 360-degree views from the viewing platform. A cast-iron bridge leads to the charming Largo do Carmo with the eponymous ruined monastery of Igreja do Carmo → p. 40 and a couple of pleasant cafés.

3 EXPLORE ALFAMA

Alfama, Lisbon's oldest neighbourhood, is a maze of steep steps and crooked alleyways, cosy nooks and crannies and decaying masonry. For centuries, the old Moorish quarter was inhabited by the city's manual workers, craftsmen and families from modest backgrounds. Now there is evidence of gentrification everywhere, and artists' studios, boutiques and fancy restaurants are moving in. Take at least half a day for this walk.

Start at the Largo de Santo António. In the centre of the square is a statue of one of Lisbon's favourite saints: cast in bronze and as usual shown with the infant Jesus in his arms. Even though the saint is widely known as 'Anthony of Padua', this is his birthplace, and the small Igreja de Santo António is said to be built on the remains of his parental home. In the Museu Antóniano (Tue–Sun 10am–1pm, 2–6pm | admission free) next door everything revolves around the saint too. A little further uphill rises Lisbon's oldest church, the imposing Sé Cathedral → p. 32 with its elegant Romanesque portal. King Afonso Henriques had the church built on the foundations of a Moorish mosque. Behind the cathedral, steps lead up to the left from Rua Augusto Rosa to the Museu Teatro Romano (Tue–Sun 10am–1pm, 2–6pm | free admission). Roman ruins have been discovered here: a theatre from the time of Emperor Nero (AD57). At the upper exit, take Rua da Saudade to the left behind the excavation site, and through the Rua de Bartolomeu Gusmão to reach the fortified walls of the Castelo de São Jorge → p. 29. A bailey surrounds the medieval citadel; the city and the Tagus spread out below.

Crossing the Largo Contador Mor, head downhill to the ⚜ Miradouro de Santa Luzia → p. 33. The stunning terrace, with its purple bougainvilleas, offers lovely views across a sea of Alfama rooftops. A little further up, on the Largo das Portas do Sol, a statue of the official patron saint of Lisbon, São Vicente, watches over the city, holding a caravel in his arms. Behind him, the two towers of his monastery, São Vicente de Fora → p. 32, rise on the skyline, while to the right is the dazzlingly white dome of the Panteão Nacional → p. 31.

Along the old Arab wall of Cerca Moura walk down the steps of Rua Norberto Araújo into the maze of alleyways that make up Alfama. Here, the houses are decorated with pots of colourful geraniums, canaries chirrup in their tiny cages, and washing blows in the breeze. Carry on downhill via the Rua da Adiça to the Largo de São Rafael to find the remains of the Torre de São Pedro de Alfama, once an entrance gate to the Moorish city. Just below here, the Judiaria is one of the former Jewish neighbourhoods of Lisbon. A few paces along, the small church of São Miguel appears, on the Largo of the same name. The Rua de São Pedro leads to Largo Chafariz de Dentro and the pink Casa/Museu do Fado → p. 29.

The Rua Terreiro do Trigo leads back into the city centre. Halfway along the street you'll pass the Chafariz d'El Rei (Old King's Fountain). Once, people would wait in line at the six pumps strictly according to social position, gender and ethnicity. Further along, on the Campo de Cebola (Field of Onions), the ship cooks would buy vegetables; the weekly slave market was held nearby. The conspicuous Casa dos Bicos → p. 29 dates from the heyday of the colonial era. Rua Alfândega leads past a lovely

Luso-Japanese café and the resplendent portal of the Manueline church of Igreja Conceição Velha. If choosing the Rua dos Bacalhoeiros to return to the centre, take a peek at the shop selling canned fish, the INSIDER TIP *Conserveira* (No. 34). The vintage-style tins of fish are colourful and lovely to look at; they make cheap and cheerful souvenirs.

heading up the first steep, cobbled street, requiring riders to lean forward a fair bit. Soundlessly, the Segways glide through the daily life of the Alfama neighbourhood, often followed by the jealous gaze of tourists exploring it on foot. The owners of the small shops and elderly residents sitting outside their houses return friendly greetings.

Two unusual façades: the Casa dos Bicos and its neighbour

4 SEGWAY THROUGH THE OLD TOWN

This slightly different tour through Alfama takes place on Segways, the self-balancing, emission-free, two-wheel personal transport device favoured by the Lisbon police. This tour is a good introduction to the Old Town.

The whole thing starts with an introduction at the Red Tour office → p. 103 in the Baixa and a training session on Praça do Comércio → p. 37. After making friends with your Segway, a short ride through the Baixa leads past Fernando Pessoa's favourite café, before

If a delivery van or a small construction site blocks the way, the route is simply changed a little bit. Sights such as the Sé Cathedral and the Panteão Nacional line the route. A slightly more challenging ramp leads into the pretty and un-crowded Miradouro de Sao Estévão, a viewpoint above the rooftops of Alfama and the river. It is possible to follow your itinerary on the (optional) GPS system with integrated audioguide.

Daily from 10am | 1 hr 15 min. | from 34 euros as part of a group, up to 49 euros for individual bookings | Rua dos Fanqueiros 18 | www.redtoursgps.com

TRAVEL WITH KIDS

FUNCENTER (118 A2–3) (𝄞 O)
Covered fairground with rollercoaster, dodgems, merry-go-round and a large garden on the upper floor of the Colombo shopping centre. *Mon–Fri noon–midnight, Sat, Sun 11am–4pm | from 1.80 euros/ride or 1 hour 10 euros | Av. Lusiada | www.funcenter.pt | Metro (blue) Colégio Militar/Luz*

JARDIM BORDALLO PINHEIRO (119 F2) (𝄞 O)
The garden of the City Museum is filled with colourful animal sculptures inspired by legendary artist Rafael Bordalo Pinheiro (honoured in the museum opposite the garden). Monkeys hang in the trees, snails creep up walls. The (real) peacocks don't know what to make of all this! *Tue–Sun 10am–1pm, 2–6pm | free admission | Campo Grande 245 | www.museudacidade.pt | Metro (yellow, green) Campo Grande*

JARDIM ZOOLÓGICO (119 D5) (𝄞 O)
Around 2200 animals live in this historic zoo. New arrivals include the cheetahs. There is also a fairground and a fun funicular. *Daily 10am–7pm, March–Sept to 8pm | admission 17 euros, children 3–11 years 12.50 euros | Estrada de Benfica 158–160 | www.zoo.pt | Metro (blue) Jardim Zoológico*

MUSEU DA CARRIS (128 B4) (𝄞 G11)
The tram museum has historic trams and buses, as well as conductor uniforms, timetables and photographs. A ride on an ancient tram is an added treat. *Mon–Sat 10am–5pm | admission 2.50 euros, children up to the age of 12 1.25 euros, family ticket 4 euros | Rua 1º de Maio 101 | www.carris.pt | eléctrico 15 to Santo Amaro*

MUSEU DA MARIONETA (130 A5) (𝄞 K10)
Marionettes, puppets and masks from all over the world, housed in a restored monastery. *Tue–Sun 10am–1pm, 2–5.30pm | admission 4 euros, children up to 5 years 1 euro, up to 14 years 2.50 euros | Rua da Esperança, 146 | www.museudamarioneta.pt | eléctrico 25 to Santos-o-Velho*

OCEANÁRIO ● (117 F4) (𝄞 S3)
The huge seawater aquarium houses around 15,000 marine-dwelling creatures. Particularly impressive is the main tank – a gigantic cylinder of glass. *Summer 10am–8pm, winter 10am–7pm | admission 12 euros, children 4–12 years 6 euros, family ticket 29 euros | www.oceanario.pt | Metro (red) Oriente*

In Lisbon children are spoilt for choice: parks and beaches, the zoo or a gigantic aquarium

PARQUE DAS NAÇÕES
(117 E/F 1–4) (*ill* S1–4)
The former Expo area has playgrounds, gardens, a 'knowledge museum' for kids, a funicular and the Oceanarium (*see above*). The *Cartão do Parque* for all sights costs 17.50 euros, children 9 euros. *Park: free admission | www.portaldasnacoes.pt | Metro (red) Oriente*

PARQUE SERAFINA
(124 B–C2) (*ill* G5–6)
Adventure playgrounds, picnic areas, and a restaurant on the edge of the huge Monsanto Park. *April–Sept daily 9am–8pm, Oct–March 9am–6pm | admission free | bus 70 from Sete Rios/Jardim Zoológico (Metro blue) to Parque Recreativa Serafina*

PISCINA OCEÁNICA (134 B4) (*ill* O)
Seawater pools, big and small, on Oeiras beach, just outside the city. *June–mid-Sept Mon–Fri 10am–7pm, Sat/Sun 9.30am–8pm | day pass 9.50 euros, chil-*dren 5–6 euros, weekends 12.50 euros, children 6.50–7.50 euros, incl. umbrellas and deckchairs | Praia Torre | train from Cais do Sodré to Santo Amaro (20 min.), then 2km/1.2mi on foot/taxi*

PLANETÁRIO C. GULBENKIAN
(126 B5) (*ill* C11)
The planetarium's Sunday stargazing sessions for children are a great hit. The commentary is all in Portuguese, but the star projection in the large dome is worth seeing even if you can't understand what is being said. *Sun 11.30am | admission free | Belém, Praça do Império | www.planetario.online.pt | eléctrico 15 to CCB*

TEATRO POLITEAMA (130 C3) (*ill* M8)
At weekends, children's musicals by the legendary Filipe La Féria are put on here. *Sat/Sun 3pm | admission 7.50–12.50 euros | Rua Portas de Santo Antão 109 | www.teatro-politeama.comt | Metro (blue) Restauradores*

FESTIVALS & EVENTS

The city on the Tagus loves to party, and there are plenty of occasions for lisboetas to celebrate something or other all year round. The biggest party month is June, when Lisbon's many popular saints are honoured.

1 Jan (*Ano Novo*, New Year), **Carnival Tuesday** (*Carnaval/Entrudo*), **Good Friday** (*Sexta-feira Santa*), **Easter Sunday** (*Páscoa*), **25 April** (*Dia da Liberdade*, Day of Freedom, honouring the 1974 Carnation Revolution), **1 May** (*Dia do Trabalhador*, Labour Day), **Whitsun** (*Pentecostes*), **Corpus Christi** (*Corpo de Deus*), **10 June** (*Dia de Portugal/ Dia de Camões*, Portuguese national holiday), **15 Aug** (*Assunção de Nossa Senhora*, Assumption of Mary), **5 Oct** (*Dia da República*, Day of the Republic), **1 Nov** (*Todos-os-Santos*, All Saints), **1 Dec** (*Dia da Restauração*, Portugal's independence from Spain 1640), **8 Dec** (*Imaculada Conceição*, Immaculate Conception), **25 Dec** (*Natal*, Christmas). On public holidays most museums, banks and shops are closed.

FESTIVALS & EVENTS

APRIL

25 April: ▶ *Parade* of the Communist Party of Portugal (PCP) along Avenida da Liberdade

Late April: ▶ *Dias da música*, three-day classical music concert marathon at the Centro Cultural de Belém, *www.ccb.pt*

Late April (10 days): ▶ *IndieLisboa*, international festival of independent film, *www.indielisboa.com*

MAY

Sun following 4 May: ▶ *Procissão de Nossa Senhora de Saúde*, procession of Our Dear Lady of Health through Mouraria, commemorating the end of the plague epidemic of 1580

Early May: ▶ *Feira do Livro*, book fair in the Parque Eduardo VII; afternoons, Fri–Sun to 11pm, *www.feiradolivrodelisboa.pt*, Metro (blue, yellow) Marquês de Pombal

JUNE/JULY

12 June: ▶ *Casamentos de Santo António*, couples from disadvantaged backgrounds can have their nuptials sponsored by the city. In the Sé and the Câmara Municipal (city hall) from 2pm

Jazz, pop and classical music festivals alleviate recent holiday cuts – but Lisbon's saints give rise to the biggest parties ...

13 June: ▶ *Dia de Santo António*
24 June: ▶ *Dia de São João*
29 June: ▶ *Dia de São Pedro*
For nearly the entire month, the so-called ▶ *Arraials* are celebrated: evening street parties with music and dance, grilled sardines and a lot of wine. For a hip neighbourhood INSIDER TIP▶ *Arraial* with less of a scrum, check out the one in Mouraria *(www.renovaramouraria.pt)*. One of the highlights: the ▶ *Marchas populares* parades on the eve of the Dia de Santo António; *from 9pm Avenida da Liberdade*

▶ *Lisboa em festa*, exhibitions, markets and concerts. *www.egeac.pt* and *www.cm-lisboa.pt*
Early July: ▶ *Delta Tejo*, three days of world music in Monsanto Park, *www.deltatejo.com*
Early July: ▶ *Sintra Festival*, two-week festival of classical music and dance in the palaces and castles of Sintra and Queluz, *www.cm-sintra.pt*
Mid-July: ▶ *Superbock Superrock*, rock festival in the Restelo stadium, *www.super bock.pt*
Mid-July: ▶ *Optimus Alive*, three-day rock festival on the banks of the Tagus in the Oeiras suburb, *www.optimusalive.com*
July: ▶ *Festival Cool Jazz*, open-air jazz concerts around Cascais, *www.cool jazzfest.com*

AUGUST
Early Aug: ▶ *Jazz em Agosto*, international jazz festival (10 days) attracting high-calibre performers, *www.musica.gulbenkian.pt/jazz/*

NOVEMBER
mid-Nov: ▶ *Arte Lisboa*, European art fair at the Parque das Nações, *www.artelisboa.fil.pt*

DECEMBER
Early Dec: ▶ *Maratona de Lisboa*, marathon through the city, *www.lisbon-marathon.com*

LINKS, BLOGS, APPS & MORE

LINKS

▶ www.streetartportugal.com The graffiti scene is very active in Lisbon, and this page presents some of the best of the crop, such as the constantly changing *Wall of Fame* near the Amoreiras shopping centre and the Kronos monster creations of Brazilians Os Gemeos on the Avenida Fontes Pereira de Melo

▶ http://timeout.sapo.pt/ Although in Portuguese only, the site of the hip Time Out city magazine is the one to check if you want to feel the pulse of the city – dates and times are international, and there's always Google Translate...

▶ www.babbel.com Portuguese online language course (no software download required), with free training app

▶ http://www.3djournal.com/001/gal_Lisabon_3D.php Impressive three-dimensional photographs of Lisbon. Even better if you still have a pair of 3D-glasses hanging around from your latest cinema visit

▶ www.camillawatsonphotography.net Website with photo gallery run by a socially committed English photographer who contributes to the revitalisation of the old Moorish quarter of Mouraria with various projects, including a portrait gallery of her neighbours on the house walls around her atelier and pinhole photography classes for children

▶ www.fatialisboa.com Information on the cool events run by Slice of Alfama, usually on Sunday afternoons till the small hours. They include photowalks, dance workshops, films and jam sessions in bohemian bars

BLOGS & FORUMS

▶ www.golisbon.com/blog Continually updated and always interesting blog on nightlife, gastro scene, etc. by a lisboeta originally from New York

▶ www.inlovewithlisbon.com Wide-ranging blog by a Lisbon lover – including a long list of more blogs: *Blogroll,*

Regardless of whether you are still preparing your trip or already in Lisbon: these addresses will provide you with more information, videos and networks to make your holiday even more enjoyable

VIDEOS

▶ http://www.youtube.com/watch?v=pZonZntFU7Y Famous agit-prop band *Homens da Luta* (Men of Struggle), who fought valiantly but unsuccessfully for Portugal in the Eurovision Song Contest 2011, sings about corruption, recession, debts and the Portuguese urge to keep buying new cars with the refrain 'e o povo, pá?' ('So what about the people, then?')

▶ http://www.youtube.com/watch?v=e2TTA-wFmoo Basejumper Mario Pardo, 'Bird Man', jumps off the highest pillar of the 25 April Bridge, surprising the participants of the Lisbon half marathon in 2009. Here with animated soundtrack

▶ http://www.youtube.com/watch?v=TiELQXT1s8Y&feature=player_embedded#! 'Lisbon is not the Perfect City' – the band *Deolinda* uses traditional Portuguese music, charged with up-to-date references, to sing the Lisbon blues

APPS

▶ Lisbon Guide Good-value iPhone-App by the tried-and-tested *Spotted By Locals community (www.spottedbylocals.com):* Lisboners old and new enthusiastically share the gems they find – restaurants, markets, parks, shops, etc. The local spotters also offer a blog and a mobile city guide

▶ Soundwalk A soundwalk iPhone app for Lisbon, allowing you to discover the sounds, noises and voices of the city with Lisbon lover John Malkovich as presenter is in production

NETWORKS

▶ www.couchsurfing.org Lisbon's Couchsurfing community is active and friendly. It includes many sub-groups for activities, language exchange and much more. This is also where you'll find the co-author of this guidebook (username: KATHLEENLX)

▶ http://www.expat-blog.com/en/network/europe/portugal/lisbon/ It's not too difficult to establish contact with lisboetas, but those staying longer may want to exchange impressions and ideas with other expats. This is the platform to find them

TRAVEL TIPS

ARRIVAL

🚗 Driving to Lisbon is really only recommended if Lisbon is a stop-over on a longer trip. Less tiring, if much more expensive, are car trains. The green insurance card is obligatory. Driving around the city can be pretty stressful: there is little street parking and traffic is heavy. Taxis are cheap here, and the urban transport system will take you to most places.

🚆 Taking the train from London to Paris (*www.cp.pt*, *www.seat61.com*), and from there to Hendaye/Irun and on by Sul-Express to Lisbon for an early-morning arrival, has its charm and is the eco option, but it is costly (approx. 400 euros) and time-consuming (about 24 hrs.). Those who are able to combine visiting Lisbon with other European stops are well served by an InterRail ticket.

🚌 Eurolines serves Lisbon from London. The journey takes around 36 hours and costs around 100 pounds. *www.eurolines.co.uk*

✈ Many airlines serve Lisbon on non-stop services. With a bit of luck, you'll find a flight for as little as 80 pounds *(easyJet, bmibaby, Thomson)*. Flight time is approx. 2.5 hrs. Flights from Boston *(SATA)* or New York *(United, TAP)* cost from 600 dollars upwards and take around 6.5 hrs. Portela airport is situated approx. 10km north of the city centre. *Shuttlebus (No. 91) into the city: 7am–11pm every 20 minutes | 3.50 euros (outside Arrivals)*. The ticket is valid for use on any bus on the day of arrival. A taxi into the city centre costs around 12 euros, meaning the taxi vouchers for sale at the tourist info in the arrivals hall for 21 euros are not exactly a good deal. However, there are rip-off taxi drivers, so you're best off heading for the taxi rank outside Departures *(Partidas)*.

BANKS & CREDIT CARDS

Opening times: Mon–Fri 8.30am–3pm. Use your direct debit or credit card to draw money from cashpoints *(Multibanco)*. Foreign credit cards are usually only accepted in major stores, restaurants, hotels, etc. Small shops and taxi drivers sometimes have difficulties providing change for 50-euro notes: não tenho troco means 'I don't have change'.

CAR HIRE

All the major providers *(Hertz, Avis*, etc.) are present in Lisbon; one money-saving choice is InterRent inside the Santa Apolónia train station *(www.interrent com)*. A national driving licence is suffi cient, but be aware of not just the obliga

RESPONSIBLE TRAVEL

It doesn't take a lot to be environmentally friendly whilst travelling. Don't just think about your carbon footprint whilst flying to and from your holiday destination but also about how you can protect nature and culture abroad. As a tourist it is especially important to respect nature, look out for local products, cycle instead of driving, save water and much more. If you would like to find out more about eco-tourism please visit: *www.ecotourism.org*

tory seat belt, but also the obligation to carry a fluorescent vest. Penalties for offences are high! Speed limits: on country roads 90km/h (55mph), on motorways 120km/h (75mph), for those who have had their permit for less than a year 90km/h (55mph). Drink-driving limit: 0.5. 24-hour breakdown service: ACP *(Automóvel Clube de Portugal) | tel. 7 07 50 95 10.*

CITY TOURS

BIKEIBERIA

Friendly bike tours through the city. *Largo Corpo Santo 5 | tel. 2 13 47 03 47 | www. bikeiberia.com*

CARRISTUR

City tours aboard a historic tram (with English-language audioguide) or by open double-decker bus. *Daily from about 10am | from 15 euros | Praça do Comércio | tel. 213 59 23 34 | www. carristur.pt*

LISBONWALKER

Relaxed city walks with locals (various languages). *Daily from 10am | from 15 euros | Praça do Comércio, corner Rua do Arsenal/Rua Aurea | tel. 2 18 86 18 40 | www.lisbonwalker.com*

INSIDER TIP ▸ FREE TOURS ◉

Every day, a couple of multilingual freelance guides wait for punters at the Camões statue. Officially what they offer are free tours, but the service can only run on tips, of course, and a guide's enthusiasm and knowledge should be rewarded. *Free city tours usually Mon–Fri 11am and 3pm. Meeting point Largo de Camões | Duration: 2.5–3 hours*

RED TOUR

Fun tours by buggy or Segway, both self-guided and accompanied. *Rua dos Fanqueiros 18 | Daily from 10.30am | from 25 euros | tel. 9 10 80 20 00 | www. redtourgps.com*

TRANSTEJO ◉

Atmospheric cruise on the Tagus (English audioguide). *April–Oct daily 3pm from Terreiro do Paço (20 euros incl. drink) or 4.30pm from Cais do Sodré (15 euros) | tel. 2 18 82 46 71 | www.transtejo.pt*

CURRENCY CONVERTER

£	€	€	£
1	1.10	1	0.90
3	3.30	3	2.70
5	5.50	5	4.50
13	14.30	13	11.70
40	44	40	36
75	82.50	75	67.50
120	132	120	108
250	275	250	225
500	550	500	450

$	€	€	$
1	0.70	1	1.40
3	2.10	3	4.20
5	3.50	5	7
13	9.10	13	18.20
40	28	40	56
75	52.50	75	105
120	84	120	168
250	175	250	350
500	350	500	700

For current exchange rates see www.xe.com

CONSULATES & EMBASSIES

UK EMBASSY
Rua de São Bernardo | 331249-082 | tel. 8 08 20 35 37 | Mon–Fri 9am–1pm and 2.30–5pm | http://ukinportugal.fco.gov.uk/en/

US EMBASSY
Avenida das Forças Armadas | 1600-081 Lisboa | tel. 2 17 27 33 00 | Mon–Fri 8am–5pm | http://portugal.usembassy.gov/index.html

CUSTOMS

Within the EU, tourists may freely import and export goods for personal use, incl. as a guideline: 800 cigarettes, 10 litres spirits and 90 litres wine. North American citizens are subject to much lower allowances, and be aware that carrying personal defence sprays and other arms is illegal in Portugal.

EMERGENCY

Police, accidents, medical emergencies: *tel. 112* (national)

HEALTH

The EHIC European health insurance card is valid in Portugal. Embassies and airlines have lists of English-speaking doctors, though most Portuguese medical staff will speak English. Accident & Emergency: *Hospital de São José | Rua José António Serrano | tel. 2 18 84 10 00 | Metro: Martim Moniz*

INFORMATION

UK PORTUGUESE TOURIST BOARD
11, Belgrave Square | London, SW1X 8PP | tel. 020 72 01 66 66 | www.visitportugal.com

US PORTUGUESE TOURIST BOARD
590 Fifth Avenue, Fourth Floor | New York, NY 10036-4704 | www.visitportugal.com

TURISMO DE LISBOA
Rua do Arsenal, 23 | tel. 2 10 31 27 00 | www.visitlisboa.com

INFORMATION IN LISBON

The Turismo hotline, *tel. 8 08 78 12 12*, provides (in English, too, for the cost of a local call) all information on hotels, public transport, etc. *Mon–Fri 8am–7pm*

TOURIST INFORMATION (TURISMOS)
– *Palácio Foz | Praça dos Restauradores | tel. 2 13 64 33 14 | www.askmelisboa.com | daily 9am–8pm | Metro (blue) Restauradores*
– *Airport Arrivals | tel. 2 18 45 06 60 | daily 7am–midnight*
– *Santa Apolónia Station | Terminal Internacional | tel. 2 18 82 16 06 | Mon–Sat 8am–1pm*
– *Lisboa Welcome Center | Praça do Comércio | tel. 2 10 31 28 10 | daily 9am–8pm | Metro (blue) Terreiro do Paço*

INTERNET

Official website of the Lisbon tourist info: *www.visitlisboa.com*; information, city maps, webcams, etc.: *www.cm-lisboa.pt*; holiday apartments and private rooms in and around Lisbon: *www.citysiesta.com, www.athomeinlisbon.com*; Hotel guide: *www.maisturismo.pt*; 360-degree panoramic views: *www. 360portugal.com*; events calendar published by the municipal culture department: *www.agendalx.pt*; cinema listings by daily newspaper Publico: *cinecartaz.publi co.pt*; English language newspaper from Portugal: *www.the-news.net*; Lisbon's hip city mag (in Portuguese): *www.timeout.pt*

INTERNET CAFÉS

ESPAÇO FÁBULAS (131 D5) (🕮 M10)
Bar, bistro, gallery, free Wi-Fi. *Mon–Wed 10am–midnight, Thu–Sat 10am–1am, Sun to 8pm | Calçada Nova de São Francisco, 14 | www.fabulas.pt | Metro (blue, green) Baixa-Chiado*

WWW.CYBERBICA.COM (130 C5) (🕮 M10)
Mon–Fri 11am–midnight | Rua Duques de Bragança, 7 | | Metro (blue, green) Baixa-Chiado

PERSONAL SAFETY

Compared to other European countries, the crime rate in Portugal remains low, but it is rising. The major touristic attractions attract pickpockets, and that's particularly true for tram No. 28!

PHONE & MOBILE PHONE

Credifon cards can be purchased from any post office and in stationery and tobacco shops. For your mobile phone, the best policy is to buy a local prepaid SIM card, to avoid paying for incoming calls. Smaller shops, often run by Indians or Nepalese, are helpful if you need advice on unlocking your device, if your own provider can't help. Always a cheaper option than calling are text messages, SMS. Checking voicemails is usually very expensive, so it's best to switch off the mailbox straight away!
Tel. dialling code for Portugal: 00351; for UK from Portugal: 0044; for Ireland 00353; for USA: 001. There are no regional dialling codes in Portugal. Directory Enquiries: 118

POLICE

The police station serving tourists *(PSP-Esquadra de Turismo)* stays open 24 hours, and English is spoken. *Tel. 21 34 21 62 3 | Palácio Foz | next to the Turismo on Praça dos Restauradores | Metro (blue) Restauradores*

POST

Opening times of the post offices: *Mon–Fri 9am–6pm.* Main post office at *Praça dos Restauradores: Mon–Fri 8am–10pm, Sat/Sun 9am–6pm.* Stamps *(selos)* can also be bought in some tobacco shops, at machines and in hotels. Letters are *cartas*, postcards *postais.* Postage for letters as well as cards within Europe is 68 cents, 80 to North America. Letterboxes are red, Express mail (Correio Azul) blue. A postcard to Britain will take around 5 days, slightly longer for North America.

BUDGETING

Wine	6–8 £ / 10–12.50 $	*for a bottle of house wine*
Eléctrico	1.20 £ / 1.80 $	*for a single trip*
Espresso	0.50 £ / 0.75 $	*for a cup*
Cake	0.80 £ / 1.25 $	*for a custard cream tart*
CD	9.50 £ / 14.50 $	*CD of Portuguese music*
Fado	16 £ / 25 $	*minimum consumption in a major fado venue*

PUBLIC TRANSPORT

CARRIS runs the city buses, *eléctricos and elevadores.* Purchased on board, a *bilhete* (ticket) costs 1.50 euros, 3.50 for the elevadores, so a daily ticket is well worth getting. Network maps are displayed at bus stops or accessible online at *www.carris.pt.* Running between 6.30am and

1am, the Metro (three lines) is fast and (outside rush hour) comfortable. A journey within the city centre costs 90 cents. *www.metrolisboa.pt*

The easiest and cheapest way to get around are combined tickets *(zapping)* for all means of transport. The *7-colinas* or *Viva Viagem* card costs 0.50 euros and is available from Metro stations and post offices, where you can also have your card charged. A daily travel card costs 3.95 euros. The machines at the Metro stations are easier to use than it might appear and have instructions in English; at most stations, staff are also on hand to help.

The *Turismos* promote and sell the *Lisboa Card*, which includes use of all public transport and free or discounted entry to museums and sights. The *Lisboa Card* costs 17.50 euros for 24 hours, 29.50 euros for 48, and 36 for 72 hrs. Have a good think about your itinerary though: the *Lisboa Card* is only really worth getting if you plan to visit a lot of museums (also remember than many museums offer free admission on Sunday mornings and most are closed on Mondays). Info: *www.askmelisboa.com*.

Passenger ferries run every 20–30 minutes from about 5.30am to 2am. Ferry terminals: Cais do Sodré, Terreiro do Paço and Belém. Ticket prices for a trip across the Tagus range between 95 cents and 2.25 euros. *www.transtejo.pt.*

Suburban trains *(Comboio suburbano)*: trains to Estoril/Cascais leave every 20

WEATHER IN LISBON

	Jan	Feb	March	April	May	June	July	Aug	Sept	Oct	Nov	Dec
Daytime temperatures in °C/°F												
	14/57	15/59	17/63	20/68	21/70	25/77	27/81	28/82	26/79	22/72	17/63	15/59
Nighttime temperatures in °C/°F												
	8/46	8/46	10/50	12/54	13/55	15/59	17/63	17/63	17/63	14/57	11/52	9/48
Sunshine hours/day												
	5	6	6	9	10	11	12	11	9	8	6	5
Precipitation days/month												
	11	8	11	7	7	2	1	1	4	7	9	11
Water temperature in °C/°F												
	14/57	14/57	14/57	15/59	16/61	17/63	18/64	19/66	19/66	18/64	16/61	15/59

minutes from Cais do Sodré. Ticket 1.80 euros. The journey to Cascais (via other stops with beach facilities, including the surfing resort of Carcavelos) lasts approx. 35 minutes. Trains to Sintra depart every 20 min. from the Rossio train station, journey time

Tickets for arts and sports events are available from the following sales points: *ABEP Kiosk | Praça dos Restauradores, Av. da Liberdade (near main post office and*

Tagus Ferry in front of the city silhouette

45 min., ticket 3.85 euros, *www.cp.pt.* Buses run by *TST (www.tsuldo tejo.pt)* take sunseekers and surfers to Costa da Caparica, the starting point for miles and miles of beaches; departures from Praça Espanha (no. 153) and Areeiro (No. 161), The return journey costs about 7.50 euros, or much cheaper if bought as a carnet.

Turismo) | Metro (blue) Restauradores; Fnac | Armazéns do Chiado | daily 10am–10pm | www.fnac.pt | Metro (blue, green) Baixa-Chiado

TAXI

Lisbon's taxis are beige in colour or black with a green roof. If the place you want to go to is not a well-known destination, make sure you have not only the address, but also a rough idea of where it is, or even better, a map. Call a taxi: *Radio Taxis de Lisboa | tel. 2 18 11 90 00*

TIME

Portugal runs on Greenwich time, i.e. British and Irish visitors don't need to set their watches.

TIPPING

While tipping is not a big part of Portuguese culture, a *gorjeta* is always appreciated for service. At restaurants, this ranges between 5 and 10% of the amount.

WI-FI

Portugal Telecom (PT) is the major service provider for public Wi-Fi. Apart from in the Baixa-Chiado Metro Station, access is payable. Buy a card (voucher) at PT stores or online from *www.ptwifi. pt.* There are often hotspots at post offices. Jardins digitais — free hotspots in parks and at miradouros are being tested.

NOTES

MARCO POLO TRAVEL GUIDES

- PACKED WITH INSIDER TIPS
- BEST WALKS AND TOURS
- FULL-COLOUR PULL-OUT MAP
  AND STREET ATLAS

USEFUL PHRASES PORTUGUESE

PRONUNCIATION

To help you say the Portuguese words we have added a simple pronunciation guide in square brackets and an apostrophe ' before the syllable that is stressed. Note the following sounds shown in the pronunciation guide:
"zh" like the "s" in "pleasure", "ng" indicates a nasal sound at the end of a word (i.e. not with distinct consonants as in English) , e.g. "não" is shown as "nowng", "ee" as in "fee", "ai" as in "aisle", "oo" as in "zoo"

IN BRIEF

Yes/No/Maybe	sim [seeng]/não [nowng]/talvez [tal'vesh]
Please	se faz favor [se fash fa'vor]
Thank you	obrigado (m)/obrigada (f) [obri'gadoo/obri'gada]
Sorry/ Excuse me, please	Desculpa! [dish'kulpa]/Desculpe! [dish'kulp]
May I ...?/ Pardon?	Posso ...? ['possoo]/ Como? ['komoo]
I would like to ...	Queria ... [ke'ria]
Have you got ...?	Tem ...? [teng]
How much is ...	Quanto custa ...? ['kwantoo 'kooshta]
good/bad/broken/ doesn't work	bem [beng]/mal [mal]/estragado [ishtra'gadoo]/ não funciona [nowng fung'siona]
too much/much/little	demais [de'maish]/muito ['mooitoo]/pouco ['pokoo]
all/nothing	tudo ['toodoo]/nada ['nada]
Help!/Attention!/Caution!	Socorro! [soo'korroo]/Atenção! [atten'sowng]
ambulance	ambulância [amboo'langsia]
police/fire brigade	polícia [pu'lisia]/bombeiros [bom'beyroosh]
prohibition/forbidden	interdição [interdi'sowng]/proibido [prooi'bidoo]
danger/dangerous	perigo [pe'rigoo]/perigoso [peri'gosoo]

GREETINGS, FAREWELL

Good morning!/after-noon!/evening!/night!	Bom dia! [bong 'dia]/Bom dia! [bong 'dia]/ Boa tarde! ['boa 'tard]/Boa noite! ['boa 'noyt]
Hello!/Goodbye!	Olá! [o'la]/Adeus! [a'dy-oosh]
See you	Cião! [chowng]
My name is ...	Chamo-me ... ['shamoo-me]
What's your name?	Como se chama? ['komoo se 'shama] Como te chamas? ['komoo te 'shamas]
I'm from ...	Sou de ... [so de]

Falas português?

'Do you speak Portuguese?' This guide will help you to say the basic words and phrases in Portuguese

DATE & TIME

Monday/Tuesday	segunda-feira [se'goonda 'feyra]/terça-feira ['tersa 'feyra]
Wednesday/Thursday	quarta-feira ['kwarta 'feyra]/quinta-feira ['kinta 'feyra]
Friday/Saturday	sexta-feira ['seshta 'feyra]/sábado ['sabadoo]
Sunday	domingo [doo'mingoo]
today/tomorrow/ yesterday	hoje ['ozhe]/amanhã [amman'ya]/ ontem ['onteng]
hour/minute	hora ['ora]/minuto [mi'nootoo]
day/night/week	dia [dia]/noite [noyt]/semana [se'mana]
month/year	mês [meysh]/ano ['anoo]
What time is it?	Que horas são? [ke 'orash sowng]
It's three o'clock	São três horas. [sowng tresh 'orash]
It's half past three	São três e meia. [sowng tresh i 'meya]

TRAVEL

open/closed	aberto [a'bertoo]/fechado [fe'shadoo]
entrance	entrada [en'trada]
exit	saída [sa'ida]
departure/arrival	partida [par'tida]/chegada [she'gada]
toilets/restrooms/ ladies/gentlemen	sanitários [sanni'tariush]/ senhoras [sen'yorash]/ senhores [sen'joresh]
(no) drinking water	água (não) potável ['agwa (nowng) po'tavel]
Where is ...?/Where are ...?	Onde é ...? ['onde e]/Onde são ...? ['onde sowng]
left/right	à esquerda [a ish'kerda]/à direita [a dee'reyta]
straight ahead/back	em frente [eng 'frente]/para atrás ['para'trash]
bus	autocarro [auto'karroo]
stop	paragem [pa'razheng]
parking lot	estacionamento [eshtassiona'mentoo]
street map/map	mapa ['mappa]/mapa da cidade ['mappa da see'dad]
train station/ harbour/ airport	estação ferroviária [eshta'sowng ferrovi'aria]/ porto ['portoo]/aeroporto [a-eyro'portoo]
schedule/ticket	horário [o'rariyu]/bilhete [bil'yet]
single/return	só ida [so 'ida]/ida e volta ['ida i 'vollta]
train/platform	comboio [kom'boyoo]/linha ['linya]
I would like to rent ...	Gostaria de alugar ... [goshta'ria de aloo'gar]
a car/a bicycle/ a boat	um carro [oong 'karroo]/uma bicicleta [ooma bissi'kletta]/um barco [oong 'barkoo]
petrol/gas station/ petrol/gas / diesel	bomba de gasolina ['bomba de gaso'lina]/ petróleo [pe'troleo]/gasóleo [ga'soleo]
breakdown/repair shop	avaria [ava'ria]/garagem [ga'razheng]

FOOD & DRINK

Could you please book a table for tonight for four?	Se faz favor, pode reservar-nos para hoje à noite uma mesa para quatro pessoas. [se fash fa'vor, 'pode reser'varnoosh 'para 'oshe ah noit ooma 'mesa 'para 'kwatroo pe'ssoash]
The menu, please	A ementa, se faz favor. [a i'menta, se fash fa'vor]
bottle/glass	garrafa [gar'raffa]/copo ['koppoo]
salt/pepper/sugar	sal [sall]/pimenta [pi'menta]/açúcar [a'ssookar]
vinegar/oil	vinagre [vi'nagre]/azeite [a'zeite]
milk/cream/lemon	leite ['leyte]/natas ['natash]/limão [li'mowng]
with/without ice/sparkling	com [kong]/sem [seng] gelo ['zheloo]/gás [gash]
vegetarian/allergy	vegetariano/-a [vezhetari'anoo/-a]/alergia [aller'zhia]
May I have the bill, please?	A conta, se faz favor. [a 'konta, se fash fa'vor]

SHOPPING

Where can I find...?	Quero ... ['keroo]/Procuro ... [pro'kooroo]
pharmacy/chemist	farmácia [far'massia]/drogaria [droga'ria]
baker/market	padaria [pada'ria]/mercado [mer'kadoo]
shopping centre	centro comercial ['sentroo kommer'ssial]
100 grammes/1 kilo	cem gramas [seng 'grammash]/um quilo [oong 'kiloo]
expensive/cheap/price	caro ['karoo]/barato [ba'ratoo]/preço ['pressoo]
more/less	mais [maish]/menos ['menoosh]

ACCOMMODATION

I have booked a room	Reservei um quarto. [rezer'vey oong 'kwartoo]
Do you have any ... left?	Ainda tem ...? [a'inda teng]
single room	um quarto individual [oong 'kwartoo individu'al]
double room	um quarto de casal [oong 'kwartoo de ka'sal]
breakfast/ half board/ full board (American plan)	pequeno-almoço [pe'kaynoo al'mossoo]/ meia pensão ['meya pen'sowng]/ pensão completa [pen'sowng kom'pleta]
shower/sit-down bath	ducha [doosha]/banho ['banyoo]
balcony/terrace	varanda [va'randa]/terraço [ter'rassoo]
key/room card	chave ['chav-e]/cartão [kar'towng]
luggage/suitcase	bagagem [ba'gazheng]/mala ['mala]/saco ['sakoo]

BANKS, MONEY & CREDIT CARDS

bank/ATM	banco ['bankoo]/multibanco ['multibankoo]
pin code	código pessoal ['kodigoo pesso'al]
cash/ credit card	em dinheiro [eng din'yeyroo]/ com cartão de crédito [kong kar'towng de 'kreditoo]
note/coin	nota ['nota]/moeda [mo'ayda]

USEFUL PHRASES

HEALTH

doctor/dentist/ paediatrician	médico ['medikoo]/dentista [den'tishta]/ pediatra [pedi'atra]
hospital/ emergency clinic	hospital [oshpi'tal]/ urgências [oor'zhensiash]
fever/pain	febre ['feybre]/dores ['doresh]
diarrhoea/nausea	diarreia [diar'reya]/enjoo [eng'zho]
sunburn	queimadura [keyma'doora]
inflamed/injured	inflamado [infla'madoo]/ferido [fe'ridoo]
plaster/bandage	penso ['pengshoo]/ligadura [liga'doora]
tablet	comprimido [kompri'midoo]

POST, TELECOMMUNICATIONS & MEDIA

stamp/letter/postcard	selo ['seloo]/carta ['karta]/postal [posh'tal]
I'm looking for a prepaid card for my mobile	Procuro um cartão SIM para o meu telemóvel. [pro'kooroo oong kar'towng sim 'para oo meyoo tele'movel]
Where can I find internet access?	Onde há acesso à internet? ['onde a a'ssessoo a 'internet]
computer/battery/ rechargeable battery	computador [kompoota'dor]/pilha ['pilya]/ bateria [bate'ria]
internet connection	ligação à internet [liga'sowng a 'internet]

LEISURE, SPORTS & BEACH

beach/sunshade/ lounger	praia ['praya]/guarda-sol [gwarda 'sol]/ espreguiçadeira [eshpregissa'deyra]
low tide/high tide/ current	maré baixa [ma're 'baisha]/maré alta [ma're alta]/ corrente [kor'rente]

NUMBERS

0	zero ['zeroo]	20	vinte [veengt]
1	um, uma ['oong, 'ooma]	21	vinte e um ['veengt e 'oong]
2	dois, duas ['doysh, 'dooash]	30	trinta ['treengta]
3	três [tresh]	40	quarenta [kwa'renta]
4	quatro ['kwatroo]	50	cinquenta [seeng'kwengta]
5	cinco ['seengkoo]	100	cem ['seng]
6	seis ['seysh]	200	duzentos [doo'zentoosh]
7	sete ['set]	1000	mil ['meel]
8	oito ['oytoo]	2000	dois mil ['doysh meel]
9	nove ['nov]	10.000	dez mil ['desh meel]
10	dez ['desh]	½	um meio [oong 'meyoo]
11	onze ['ongs]	¼	um quarto [oong 'kwartoo]

STREET ATLAS

The green line [ ] indicates the Walking tours (p. 90–95)

All tours are also marked on the pull-out map

Photo: fountain on Rossio square

Exploring Lisbon

The map on the back cover shows how the area has been sub-divided

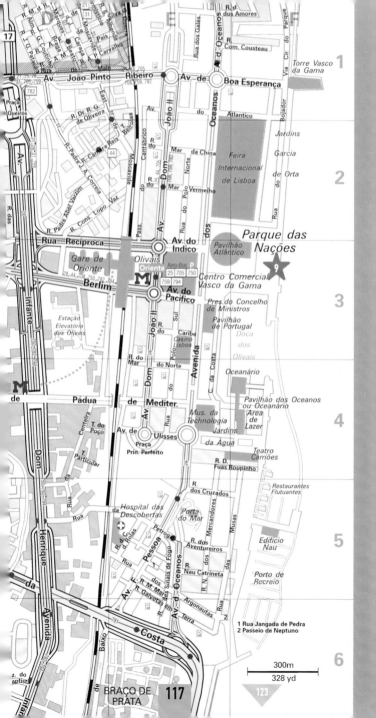

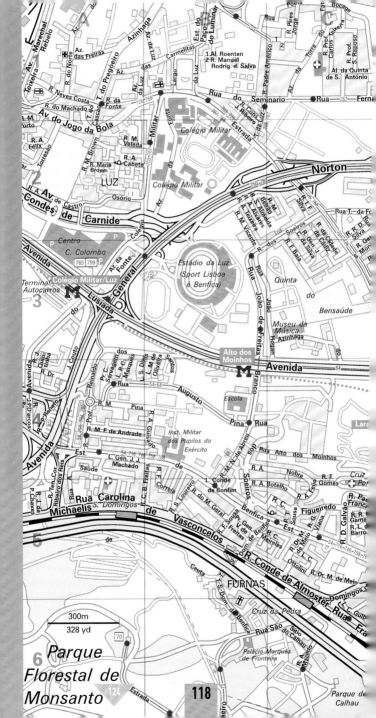

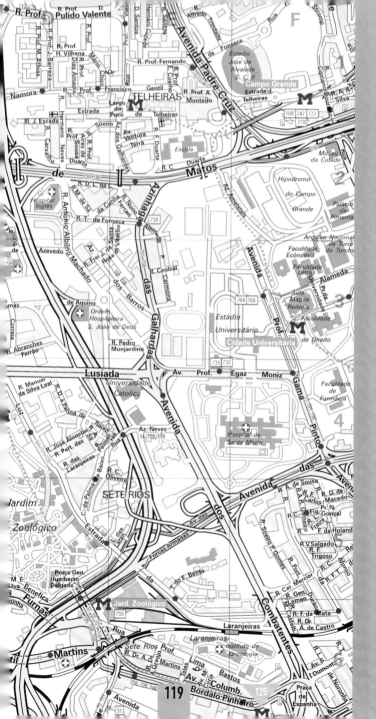

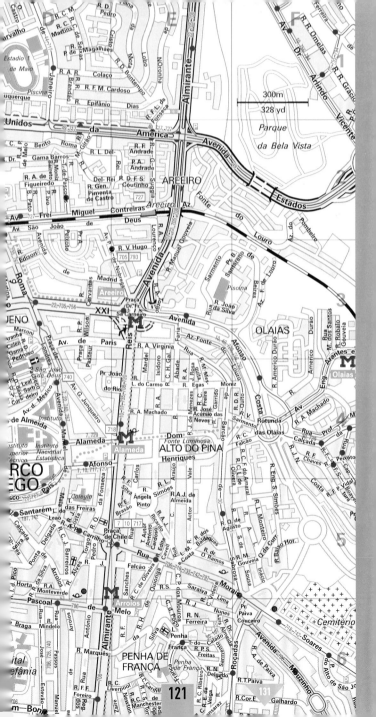

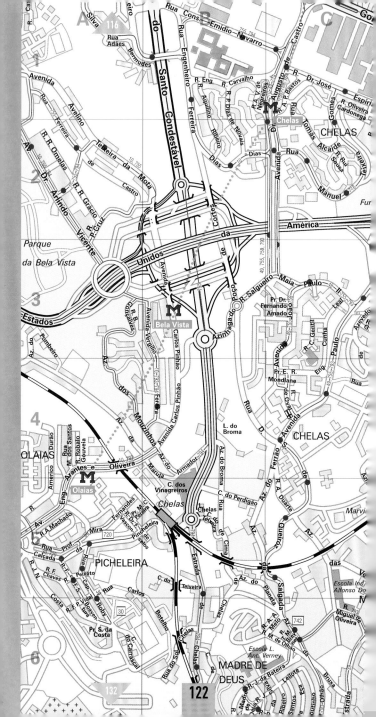

D E F

Edifício Nau

Porto de Recreio

117

1 Rua Jangada de Pedra
2 Passeio de Neptuno

Costa

BRAÇO DE PRATA

Braço de Prata

POÇO DO BISPO

Az. do Baptista

R. do Operária

R. F. Palha

R. Dr. E. de Vasconcelos

R. Matinha

R. Particular

Pedroso

R. F. M. d. Guerra

Pr. D. L. da Silva

R. Amorim

Patrocinio

793 39

Açucar

R. P. Henriques

Pr. D. L. da Silva

Centro de Apoio Social

Leitão

R. do Cap. R. A. A. Penedo

R. J. D. Barreiros

BEATO

D. do Poço do Bispo

Convento do Beato

133

123

300m
328 yd

Rua Jangada de Pedra

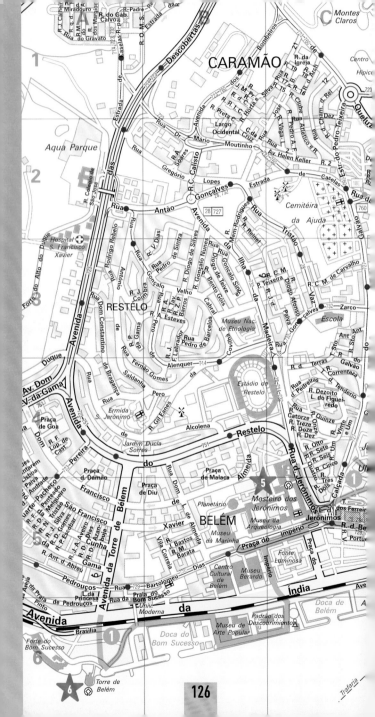

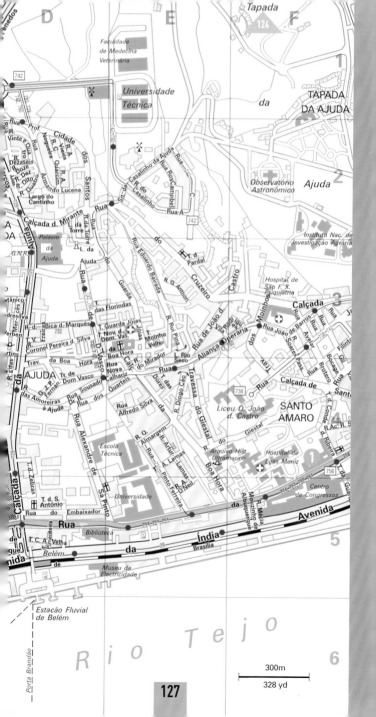

Tapada

TAPADA
DA AJUDA

D   E   F

1

Faculdade
de Medecina
Veterinária

742

Universidade
Técnica

da

Ajuda

Observatório
Astronómico

Rua Prof.
R. Vinte e Uma
tro
R. Dezasseis
doze
R. Dez
R. Oito
R. Quatro

Cidade dos Santos

R. Costa
R. Nogueira Quércm
Armando Lucena

Casalinho da Ajuda
R. do Casalinho
Rua Roy Campbell
Rua-A
Rua-A
C

2

Instituto Nac. de
Investigação Agrária

Largo do
Cantinho

Calçada d. Mirante
Rua da Torre
R. da Torre
L. da
Ajuda

Rua da Ajuda

do

Cruzeiro

Castro

G.N.R.

Palácio
da
Ajuda

Rua Eduardo Barata

T. d.
Pardal

R. G. Amboð

Hospital de
Sao F. X.
Psiquiatria

Calçada

3

tânico
dresiva
erben

R. das Florindas
Bica d. Marquês
732
T. Guarda Jóias
T. Nov. d.
Dom. Vas.
Coronel Pereira e Silva
V. Freitas
Trav. da Boa Hora
da

Rua da Guarda

R. Rui Pina

Rua de João d.
Vila Rodr.
esq.

Moinho
Velho
L. Rio
Seco

Aliança Operaria

Rua João de Barros
Rua Soares Pass.
R. Avelar

Rua

Rua

Rua Brotero

Rua

3

Trav

dos

Moinhos

AJUDA

R. G.J.P.
Fernan. Dom Vasco
das Amoreiras
à Ajuda
Dr. R.
Rua dos

Rua
Nova
Calhariz

Boa Hora
Rua
do Mirador

Rua

L. das
Dores

Travessa do Giestal

Calçada de

SANTO
AMARO

R.Ac. R. S

Sousado
Rua Alexandre de

Rua
Alfredo Silva

R.Diogo Cão
R. das Dores

da

738

Liceu D. João
d. Castro

Rua

do

Giestal

Santa

4

Escola
Técnica

R.Q. Almargem
R. Arthur Lamas
Rua-R. A. Lamas
R. Pinto Ferreira
R. A. O'Neil

Boa Hora

Arquivo Hist.
Ultramarino

Hospital de
Egas Moniz

R. Ribeira

Universidade

Sá Pinto

T. d. S.
António

Rua do Embaixador

R. Maria
Moizinho de
Albuquerque

756

Centro
de Congressos

Calçada
de
que
nida

T. Zebras
T. C. A. Velha
Belém
de

Rua

Biblioteca

Rua

da

Índia

Brasília

Avenida

5

Museu da
Electricidade

Porta Brandão

Estacão Fluvial
de Belém

R i o   T e j o

6

300m
328 yd

127

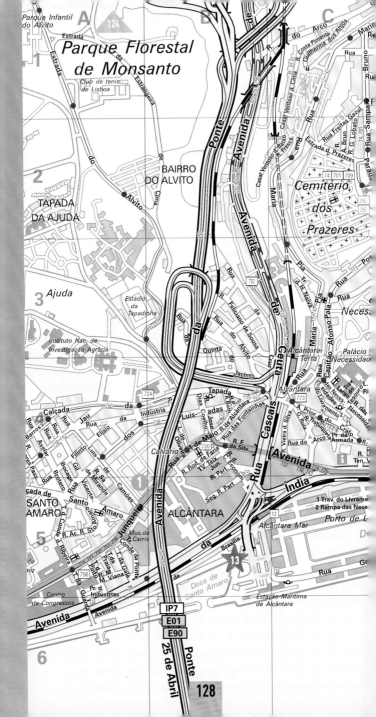

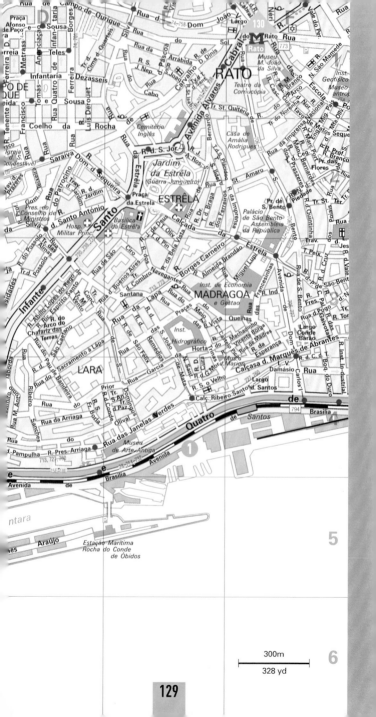

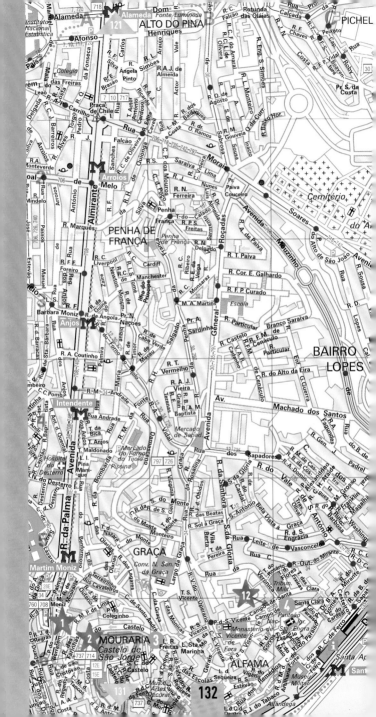

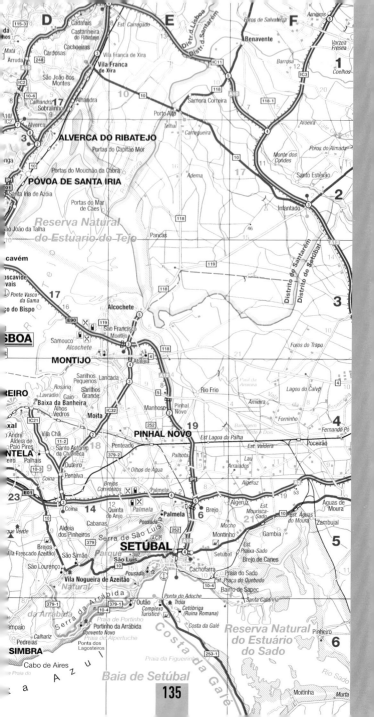

This index lists a selection of the streets and squares shown on the street atlas

KEY TO STREET ATLAS

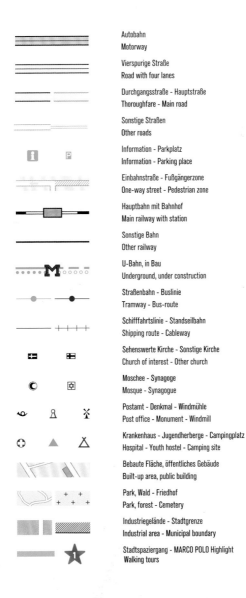

Autobahn Motorway	
Vierspurige Straße Road with four lanes	
Durchgangsstraße - Hauptstraße Thoroughfare - Main road	
Sonstige Straßen Other roads	
Information - Parkplatz Information - Parking place	
Einbahnstraße - Fußgängerzone One-way street - Pedestrian zone	
Hauptbahn mit Bahnhof Main railway with station	
Sonstige Bahn Other railway	
U-Bahn, in Bau Underground, under construction	
Straßenbahn - Buslinie Tramway - Bus-route	
Schifffahrtslinie - Standseilbahn Shipping route - Cableway	
Sehenswerte Kirche - Sonstige Kirche Church of interest - Other church	
Moschee - Synagoge Mosque - Synagogue	
Postamt - Denkmal - Windmühle Post office - Monument - Windmill	
Krankenhaus - Jugendherberge - Campingplatz Hospital - Youth hostel - Camping site	
Bebaute Fläche, öffentliches Gebäude Built-up area, public building	
Park, Wald - Friedhof Park, forest - Cemetery	
Industriegelände - Stadtgrenze Industrial area - Municipal boundary	
Stadtspaziergang - MARCO POLO Highlight Walking tours	

INDEX

This index lists all sights, museums and destinations plus the main squares and streets, the key terms and people featured in this guide. Numbers in bold indicate a main entry.

WRITE TO US

e-mail: info@marcopologuides.co.uk

Did you have a great holiday?
Is there something on your mind?
Whatever it is, let us know!
Whether you want to praise, alert us
to errors or give us a personal tip –
MARCO POLO would be pleased to
hear from you.
We do everything we can to provide
the very latest information for your trip.

Nevertheless, despite all of our authors'
thorough research, errors can creep
in. MARCO POLO does not accept any
liability for this. Please contact us by
e-mail or post.

MARCO POLO Travel Publishing Ltd
Pinewood, Chineham Business Park
Crockford Lane, Chineham
Basingstoke, Hampshire RG24 8AL
United Kingdom

PICTURE CREDITS
Cover Photograph: cathedral Sé, cable car (Huber: Gräfenhain)
Images: MG de Sant Venant (1 bottom); DuMont Bildarchiv: Widmann (68); R. Freyer (flap l., 23, 71, 76, 95); J. Holz (2 bottom, 3 top, 3 centre, 49, 56/57, 65, 66/67, 74/75); Huber: Borchi (4), Gräfenhain (1 top), Howard (12/13), Kaos (102 top), Raccanello (92), Giovanni Simeone (2 centre bottom, 26/27), Spila (2 top, 5); ©iStock-photo.com: Nikola Miljkovic (16 top); G. Jung (32/33); G. Knoll (8, 10/11, 36, 46, 51, 53, 72, 73, 98, 99); C. Lachenmaier (58); Joanna Latka: Jaime Vasconcelos (17 bottom); mauritius images: AGE (18/19, 96/97), Alamy (2 centre top, 6, 7, 15, 20, 24 r., 25, 30, 35, 38, 54, 61, 62 r., 63, 79, 89, 90/91, 96, 97, 98/99, 102 bottom, 109, 114/115), Cubolmages (87); Marco Pereira (16 bottom); Red Tour Gps Electric Move: Susana Welsh (17 top); T. Stankiewicz (9); Storytailors Atelier (16 centre); White Star: Gumm (3 bottom, 62 l., 78, 82/83, 84); T. P. Widmann (flap r., 42, 103); centre Zegers (24 l., 40, 45, 81)

1st Edition 2013
Worldwide Distribution: Marco Polo Travel Publishing Ltd, Pinewood, Chineham Business Park, Crockford Lane, Basingstoke, Hampshire RG24 8AL, United Kingdom. Email: sales@marcopolouk.com
© MAIRDUMONT GmbH & Co. KG, Ostfildern
Chief editors: Michaela Lienemann (concept, managing editor), Marion Zorn (concept, text editor)
Author: Annette Hüller, co-author: Kathleen Becker, Editor: Jochen Schürmann
Programme supervision: Anita Dahlinger, Ann-Katrin Kutzner, Nikolai Michaelis
Picture editor: Gabriele Forst
What's hot: wunder media, Munich;
Cartography street atlas: © MAIRDUMONT, Ostfildern; Cartography pull-out map: © MAIRDUMONT, Ostfildern
Design: milchhof: atelier, Berlin; Front cover, pull-out map cover, page 1: factor product munich
Translated from German by Kathleen Becker, Lisbon; editor of the English edition: Dorothy Stannard, London
Prepress: BW-Medien GmbH, Leonberg
Phrase book in cooperation with Ernst Klett Sprachen GmbH, Stuttgart, Editorial by Pons Wörterbücher

DOS & DON'TS ☝

BEING PUSHY

On the bus and tram, things are *very British:* passengers take their place in the queue. And if you don't want to risk a fit on the part of the driver, don't ever board a bus at the back! Tickets need to be validated at the front.

SAYING 'GRACIAS' FOR THANK YOU

'Thank you' in Portuguese is *obrigada* (to a lady) and *obrigado* (to a gentle-men). If you don't want to out yourself as an arrogant foreigner, don't use the Spanish *gracias* – though some young Lisboners sometimes use it jokingly.

WANDERING DARK STREETS ALONE AT NIGHT

Around the party mile of Bairro Alto and in Alfama in particular, avoid lonely lanes at night. Lisbon might be Europe's second-safest capital, but muggings do occur!

SLAGGING OFF PORTUGAL

In these difficult times of austerity measures, calling Portugal 'a Third World country' or 'an embarrassment' is the prerogative of the locals ...

TURNING UP TOO EARLY

The Portuguese sense of time could be called 'elastic'. If invited to dinner, turning up on the dot risks embarrassing your hosts. Fifteen minutes after the agreed time is a safe bet. This applies to both parties of course.

VOICING DISCONTENT LOUDLY

Stay calm if something isn't working out. The Portuguese don't share the archetypal Latin temperament, and situations can turn into a bureaucratic stone wall if you get angry. Describe what you need politely, and insist; then people will usually try to help.

LEAVING THINGS LYING AROUND

Don't leave cameras, iPhones or hand-bags lying around, on a café table, for instance. This also applies to leaving possessions on display in hire cars. It's too much of a temptation for thieves. Also watch out on buses, trams or trains or anywhere else that is crowded. Don't bring all your cards and cash, and place valuables in different pockets.

THINKING EVERYTHING'S INCLUDED

When the waiter places ham, cheese or other titbits on the table unasked, be aware that everything like this costs extra. Bread, butter and olives, however, are usually part of the couvert, which is charged no matter what.